Dietrich Bonhoeffer's
Meditations on Psalms

OTHER BOOKS IN THIS SERIES

Formerly titled *My Soul Finds Rest*

Dietrich Bonhoeffer's
Meditations on Psalms

Editor and Translator
Edwin Robertson

GRAND RAPIDS, MICHIGAN 49530 USA

ZONDERVAN™

Dietrich Bonhoeffer's Meditations on Psalms
Copyright © 2002 by Edwin Robertson
Formerly titled *My Soul Finds Rest*

Requests for information should be addressed to:

Zondervan, *Grand Rapids, Michigan 49530*

Library of Congress Cataloging-in-Publication Data

Bonhoeffer, Dietrich, 1906-1945.
    Dietrich Bonhoeffer's Meditations on Psalms / editor and translator,
Edwin Robertson. — 2nd ed.
    Rev. ed. of: My soul finds rest. c2002
    Includes bibliographical references.
       p. cm.
    ISBN-10: 0-310-26703-X
    ISBN-13: 978-0-310-26703-4
    1. Bible. O.T. Psalms—Meditations.   2. Bible. O.T. Psalms—Sermons.
3. Lutheran Church—Sermons.   4. Sermons, German—Translations into
English.   I. Robertson, Edwin Hanton.   II. Bonhoeffer, Dietrich, 1906–
1945 My soul finds rest. III. Title.
BS1430.54 .B66 2005
223'.206—dc22

                                         2005017554

All Scripture quotations, unless otherwise indicated, are taken from the *Holy Bible:
New International Version*®. NIV®. Copyright © 1973, 1978, 1984 by International Bible Society. Used by permission of Zondervan. All rights reserved.

Interior design by Beth Shagene

Printed in the United States of America

Contents

Prologue

WHEN ADOLF HITLER CAME TO POWER IN 1933, the Protestant churches in Germany largely welcomed him. There were exceptions: people like Martin Niemöller, Paul Schneider (who in 1939 became the first pastor to be put to death for his obedience to God in defiance of Nazi orders), and Dietrich Bonhoeffer.

Apart from such individuals who saw the dangers of Nazism, there was also an organized resistance by Protestant pastors who formed what they called "the Confessing Church." It was not a political resistance, which would have been foreign to a Lutheran church, but a spiritual and theological one. It was a movement to protect the church from the heretical influence of the Nazis. They were not opposing National Socialism but the unacceptable interference of the Nazis with the church and the influence of Nazi mythology on Christian beliefs. The strongest center of this resistance was in Prussia, and the strongest part of the Confessing Church came from the church of the Old Prussian Union.

Dietrich Bonhoeffer was both a pastor of this church and a strong supporter of the Confessing Church. He had gone further than most of its members in criticizing the actions of the Nazis, particularly in relation to the Jews. In 1933 he wrote a pamphlet on "The Jewish Problem," which endangered him.

For two years, he served as pastor to a German-speaking congregation in London. Then, when the Confessing Church wanted to establish a seminary for theological students intended for its ministry, they recalled Bonhoeffer to Germany to direct it, eventually in Finkenwalde near Stettin. He worked with students there from 1935 to 1937.

This was a precarious venture for all concerned. The students had already received an academic education in one or more of the German universities. By coming to Finkenwalde they were cutting themselves off from the national church, which meant sacrificing all prospect of a career in the church. The theological seminary was, in effect, illegal—unrecognized by the authorities except as a protest. It is surprising that this seminary was allowed to function as long as it did; after two years it was closed on the orders of the Gestapo.

One of Bonhoeffer's earliest lectures was "Christ in the Psalms," delivered on July 31, 1935. After a survey of the incredible range of the Psalms, he concluded: "There is not a single detail of the piety and impiety of the Christian church that is not found there." He spoke of a study of the Psalms as "a strange journey of ups and downs, falling and rising, despair and exaltation," which is the experience of those who "pray their way through the Psalms, one after the other."

Those who objected that some psalms cannot be prayed with sincerity because the Christian conscience rebelled against what they said or because they could not understand them, met a blunt reply: "The only way to understand the Psalms is on your knees, the whole congregation praying the words of the Psalms with all its strength." And to those who complained that they cannot pray what they do not understand, the equally blunt reply: "How can you understand what you have not prayed? It is not our prayer that interprets the Psalms but the Psalms that interpret our prayers." For Bonhoeffer, as for Martin Luther, the Psalms were both the Word of God and the words of men. The Psalter is both the prayer book of the Church and the prayer of God in Holy Scripture. Luther believed that you could hear the voice of Christ in every psalm—praying with us and for us.

Although Bonhoeffer begins with Luther, he brings his own life experience to bear upon his understanding of the Psalms—each event in his life impinging upon his understanding both of the relevance and the judgment of them.

In 1935, Bonhoeffer had ten more years to live an extraordinarily challenging life that taught him much about the value of the Psalms. It will be one of the purposes of this book to show the way in which he prayed and preached the Psalms as life compelled him to rethink their meaning every step of the way to his martyrdom.

When in prison at the end of his life, Bonhoeffer found comfort in Psalm 30:5: "For his anger is but for a moment, and his favor is for a lifetime. Weeping may tarry for the night, but joy comes with the morning" (RSV). When his thoughts crystallized in poetry, he could write:

Though from the old our hearts are still in pain,
while evil days oppress with burdens still,
Lord, give to our frightened souls again,
salvation and thy promises fulfilled.

Sermon to the Preachers' Seminar

Berlin, May 20, 1926

Psalm 127

ON DIETRICH BONHOEFFER'S TWENTIETH BIRTHDAY, February 4, 1926, he was a senior theology student at the University of Berlin. This was his third year. He had previously studied in Tübingen and, with his brother, taken a three-month tour of Rome and North Africa. The importance of this visit was his discovery of the power and beauty of the Roman Liturgy in Holy Week. It did nothing, however, to change his theological objections to Rome.

On May 20, he delivered the following sermon on Psalm 127 at the preachers' seminary. He was quite aware of the secluded life of the seminary and the turmoil of Berlin outside its walls, where Fascists and Communists fought in the streets. After its defeat in the Great War, Germany, a once-proud nation, had been forced to sign the hated Versailles Treaty. Inflation was rampant and unemployment had reached an unprecedented peak. An unpopular government in Weimar cared little for the church and seemed unable to govern the state. The more sober elements in the German population put their heads down and worked all hours for low pay to rebuild the nation.

Bonhoeffer found Psalm 127 to be a very timely word for a desperate nation.

PSALM 127

Unless the LORD builds the house,
its builders labor in vain.
Unless the LORD watches over the city,
the watchmen stand guard in vain.
In vain you rise early
and stay up late,
toiling for food to eat—
for he grants sleep to those he loves.

Sons are a heritage from the LORD,
children a reward from him.
Like arrows in the hands of a warrior
are sons born in one's youth.
Blessed is the man
whose quiver is full of them.
They will not be put to shame
when they contend with their enemies in the gate.

Sermon to the Preachers' Seminar

We live in a time when more than ever before we speak and must speak of building and rebuilding. We speak of how our commerce must grow and what trade agreements will bring about this result today or tomorrow, as quickly as possible. We speak of the best arrangements on workers' wages and how workers and employers alike can find a common interest in success. We ask ourselves how we can begin to become once more a rich, trouble-free, happy, and respected people. We work today as perhaps we have never worked before to achieve that goal as soon as possible. We all want to do our best to add our one stone to this building.

God knows there are others who do not think like this. Let us pray to God that he restores their sight! But we speak here only of those who use the word "building" seriously, who really put their life and their working strength into it. And of these, there truly are many, very many. Woe betide us if we are not among them!

With the question of commerce, there is another question, closely associated with it—the social question! How much this is talked about and how much is already being done! And we thank those men and women who dedicate themselves to this and do fruitful work. And every one of us here would wish to belong to this band of men and women who take seriously love of their neighbor in this work.

Woe betide our Christianity if we do not do this. The people should be rich, healthy, and strong. To this end, the scientists sit from morning to night at their benches, in their institutes, and with their apparatus. Science, technology—they all work toward building the future. Take up any newspaper and read the print or between the lines and you will hear the word, loud and clear: build, build!

So far as we speak of really serious people, they want not only to be rich and respected but a people who are healthy in body and soul. We provide the young people of our cities with opportunities to explore, to dance, and to play. We rejoice that they go out into the countryside instead of seeking their pleasures in dirty and undesirable places in the cities. We speak much more of moral rebuilding, without which nothing can happen, and know that such cannot come about unless each of us begins with his own personal moral building. There are many men and women who see their vocation in the moral training of our youth. They work at it with all their strength and do not complain but are proud of their calling. We are lucky to have such people! And should we not all, so far as we can, have at least a small part of this work? Woe betide us if it is not so! Otherwise we are truly only Sunday Christians, from 9:00 to 10:00 in the morning!

But let us hear the words of the Psalms: "Unless the
LORD builds the house . . ."

Anyone who hears these words aright sees in them
judgment over all times of frantic building and over all
times of secure possession. If only the hands of men build
and the Lord does not build, there is nothing. There are
only two things that we must fully understand: "Unless
the LORD builds" and "its builders labor in vain."

But what does it mean that God should build? Is there
on earth a building, a house, a city, that has fallen from
heaven, that was not built by men? Does this verse mean
that we have to wait until such a miracle happens? If all
our building is in vain, really in vain, which means "of no
value," why do we begin to rebuild what has been
destroyed instead of waiting for God to build? Why do
we continue to work to establish the church where once
it belonged? Why do we struggle for the moral and religious education of our children, if all we do is in vain? In
this way, many may argue if they take the words "in
vain" seriously.

And yet, another voice is raised and with comfort says:
Certainly, all our doing is in vain if we do only what we
want to do. Then we can hope for nothing. But when
we are most careful to do what God wants and not what
we want, then it is as though the Lord himself builds. For
how else can the Lord build except through us? It is only
when we build other than in the spirit of the Lord that

our very best work is in vain. People who talk like that are certainly right. Woe betide us if we do not go to work with our full strength and goodwill!

But are we really agreeing with those who say that when we build with our very best endeavor, it is the same as if the Lord builds? Must there not be with this building of the Lord another explanation than simply our piety and goodwill? None of us can doubt that many are building with the highest motives and with all their strength. Do we want then to say that here God is at work? Here, where only men are involved? Are we then to claim that so long as we have goodwill, God's action is unnecessary? Are we so blind that we do not see that all our work always carries the scars of the past, the signs of sinfulness? Do we no longer see that we are in the world and remain only with our own ideas, even the most pious of us? That we cannot do God's will unless God wills it? That we cannot say yes to God's will, if God has not said yes to us?

Yes, it is so! We fail to see the danger of raising a new Tower of Babel, from which we say that we have raised it to heaven ourselves, that now we no longer need the work of God, but our own will can take the place of that. We really believe that we have done all and enough with our work of religion and moral renewal. And we never think that there is something else to be said: "It is good," as good as we are. All we would say is, "We all want with all our heart to be a rich, happy people, and each to be a good, happy person, and have a merciful God." Ah! This is not something we can give ourselves, nor can we believe it possible by ourselves.

Let us examine ourselves seriously for once. Who would not recoil from this honest view of himself? A doubtful praise for him who has nothing to be ashamed of! Family, "kith and kin," state, church, union, and not least, development of our own "personality," these are the gods with whom we dance! Who now thinks of the One who gives meaning to everything, who speaks of judgment and grace over all this? Who now thinks that our God is a God who shatters nations like the potter's clay? And that it depends upon him whether our building is in vain or not? That it depends not on some will or skill of ours but only on God's compassion whether the light of eternity, the light of divine grace, shines upon all our sin?

Why have we forgotten this? Because the gracious God gives rain to the just and the unjust; because a building that he has not built may remain standing for a long time; and because a building that he has built may perhaps survive only for a short time.

When we humans say "in vain" we mean this world. God means eternity. That psalmist knew as well as we do that houses and cities built without God have survived in this world, and from the point of view of this world, they were not built in vain. And that the cities built by God's chosen often enough were soon destroyed.

"Unless the LORD builds the house, the builders labor in vain . . ." Not in vain for this world. The Tower of Babel was higher than all other towers. Not in vain for the commercial and "moral" health of the people. Not in vain for the terrifying rat race of the commercial struggle in the world market. In vain for eternity, in vain! For that on which the light of the rule of God does not shine is in vain. For God's grace is far from it, in vain! For God's love has not protected it.

The psalmist goes on, "Unless the LORD watches over the city . . ." Perhaps not in vain for this world, not in vain for the eyes of men, but in vain for eternity, in vain for the eyes of God! For its continued existence stands under the judgment of God, in vain! For its existence in time is its death in eternity.

But the Lord is always building for eternity, even when he is not building for time. God builds when he is gracious unto us, when he says yes to us and to our doings, to our work on ourselves, to our striving to raise the standard of our trade, health, morality, and religion; when he lets his grace shine even upon the sins of the big cities, his forgiveness over the competitive battles of the powerful of this world. The Lord blesses when he preserves for eternity that which in the coming and going of time pleases him.

It is only when God wills to look upon our person and our doing that we do not build in vain. It is only when

God lets the light of eternity fall upon us and our work that the watchman does not "stand guard in vain." God builds when he makes new people out of the old, new people for his eternal kingdom. When God says yes to us in our sin, then we are already justified, although we remain sinners. For God sees not the partial but the whole. So the light of fulfillment shines even upon our work, sinful as we are.

God's building for eternity is forgiveness, an overpowering divine love. So long as we are on this earth, we remain and our work remains full of sin, it is temporal as everything else is. But God has looked upon it, God has built it, God has forgiven. So long as we are at work, we will not build the kingdom of God. But so long as God looks upon us and our work and has compassion upon the godless, so surely will he himself build his house, the eternal kingdom, where all is spirit. God the Father will reveal his lordship. We, through Jesus Christ, his Son, have access to him and receive forgiveness of all our sins. And God will be all in all. Your kingdom come! Maranatha, yes, come Lord Jesus.[1]

Sermon to the German-Speaking Congregation

Barcelona, July 15, 1928

Psalm 62

As a THEOLOGY STUDENT, Bonhoeffer made steady, brilliant progress. The eminent theologian Karl Barth referred to his doctoral thesis as a "theological miracle"! By 1928, he had taken his first examination to qualify as a theology teacher at the university.

The family, who at first had been surprised that he had chosen theology, began to see his future as an academic theologian. They recalled that Karl Alfred von Hase, his grandfather on his mother's side, had been a church theologian and court preacher to the kaiser at Potsdam. They came to see Dietrich's future in a brighter light.

Then he surprised them again by turning away from an academic career and choosing to become a pastor. He showed great gifts with young people and liked preaching.

His first full-time appointment was to a German-speaking congregation in Barcelona. This congregation was also secluded from the privations of Berlin and the revolutionary movements in Spain. They were businessmen, mostly, with their families, living comfortably and much concerned with commercial success. Bonhoeffer saw their need for spiritual development.

He also tried to interest them in what was going on in Spain. He himself was deeply influenced by Spanish culture. He learned Spanish to read Cervantes in the original, studied children's games for echoes of old theological disputes between Christians and Muslims, and even took an interest in bullfighting.

On July 15, 1928, he preached on Psalm 62.

PSALM 62:1–8

My soul finds rest in God alone;
  my salvation comes from him.
He alone is my rock and my salvation;
  he is my fortress, I will never be shaken.

How long will you assault a man?
  Would all of you throw him down—
  this leaning wall, this tottering fence?
They fully intend to topple him
  from his lofty place;
  they take delight in lies.
With their mouths they bless,
  but in their hearts they curse.   *Selah*

Find rest, O my soul, in God alone;
  my hope comes from him.
He alone is my rock and my salvation;
  he is my fortress, I will not be shaken.
My salvation and my honor depend on God;
  he is my mighty rock, my refuge.
Trust in him at all times, O people;
  pour out your hearts to him,
  for God is our refuge.   *Selah*

Sermon to the German-Speaking Congregation in Barcelona

My soul finds rest in God alone;
my salvation comes from him.

Thousands of years ago, in a distant place, far in the East, there was an upright man who, in the storms of life, sank to his knees in the solitariness and rest of the holy Jewish temple. He absorbed it, drunk it deeply into his soul; it was his holy rest, and he was able to say, "My soul finds rest in God alone; my salvation comes from him."

O, sweet singer of our psalm, you have spread out for us the blessedness and the sweetness of the peace of God upon this earth. Like the vision of lovely dreams is your psalm, so longed for and so far, ah! so far. We love your vision.

But we no longer understand it; we no longer wish to understand it. Ah! Come near to us, come very close, in this holy hour, and tell us something of this "rest" of God, of this rest for our soul. Imprint your vision deep in our hearts and show us something of the source of your blessedness. For we know that you have much to tell us.

"My soul finds rest in God alone." That sounds like a medieval picture painted on a gold background, or some memory from childhood days, coming over to us in the twentieth century—something miraculous.

The word *soul* is strange to us. Is there anything like a soul in our days, this age of machines, of warring commercial deals, in an age when fashion and sport dominate our world? Is it not just a lovely childhood memory like so many other things? It sounds so wonderful and so strange in the shouting and confusion of voices—this little word "soul." It has such a quiet, restful sound that we can scarcely hear it above the rage and anger within us.

But it speaks the language of our greatest responsibility and deepest seriousness: You, a human being, have a soul. Take care that you do not lose it, that you do not, one day, awake from the turmoil of your life—professional as well as private—and see that within you is an emptiness, a plaything of events, a leaf tossed here and there and blown away, that you are without a soul. As a human being, take care of your soul!

What shall we say about that soul? It is the life that God has given us. It is what God has loved upon us, what he has breathed upon us out of his eternity. It is the love in us—and the longing and the holy unrest and the responsibility and the joy and the pain. It is the divine breath breathed into a mortal being. To each one of you, I say, "You have a soul." That is not a word of sweet, childish memory or dream, but real. And with it, at the same time, comes heavy, serious responsibility that is laid upon us and for which we must answer in eternity.

"My soul finds rest in God." What does that mean? It is so great and holy. Yet one must speak of it in human terms. It is like the innocent child on his mother's breast, quiet and fulfilled, with all his needs met and at rest. It is like a boy satisfied that he has seen his hero or his leader; like the crying child who feels the touch of his mother's hand on his forehead, so that all his troubles go away and he is at rest; like the girl with all her worries gone when she thinks of the coming of her first child; like the man, whose passion and unrest are stilled by the glance of his beloved; like the friend in the gaze of his true friend; like a patient at rest before the doctor; like the elderly person rested in the face of death; and like all of us, standing in reverent respect before the silence of nature beneath a starry heaven—thus should our soul be at rest from its turmoil and wildness and hate, before the eye of God.

Here all thirst is quenched. Here pleasure becomes blessedness, longing finds its fulfillment, the hectic activity of the day finds rest in the protecting shadow of God's hand, the burdens and troubles of the day fall away and become free and restful in the sight of God, shed and silenced in worship and adoration. "My soul finds rest in God."

Yes, many may say, you talk once more of beautiful things. But why do so very few of them happen? There are two simple reasons.

First, we are nervous about quietness or rest. We are so used to restlessness and noise that we feel uncomfortable in the stillness. And therefore we run away from rest, we chase from one event to another, lest, for a moment, we find ourselves face-to-face with ourselves alone. We are afraid to look at ourselves in the mirror. We are bored with ourselves. And it is often the most miserable and fruitless hour when we have to be alone with ourselves.

But it is not only fear of being with ourselves, facing up to who we are and our need to be cleansed, but far more we are afraid to be alone with God, lest he disturb our aloneness and discover us and deal with us. We fear that he will draw us into a one-to-one relationship and chide us according to his will. We are afraid of such an uncomfortable personal encounter with God, and therefore we avoid it, even dismissing thoughts about God in case he comes too near. It would be terrible to have to look God in the face and be responsible to him.

This fear is a symbol of our time. We live under the constant fear that suddenly we may be packed off to eternity. We would much rather be in company or in the cinema or at the theater until we are taken off to the grave than spend one minute with God. Ask yourself if that is not true. That is the first reason why we are afraid of silence and rest.

The second reason is that we know how poor our religious life is. Perhaps we made a start once. But how quickly we gave up. We say we are not in the mood. But religion itself provides the mood. So we wait until it comes over us. Then we wait and we wait, often for years, perhaps all our life, until we are in the mood and become religious. Behind that way of thinking lies a great deception. Very well, let us allow that religion is the stuff of mood, but God is not dependent upon mood. He is there when we are not in the mood, drawing us into closeness with him.

Does that thought not worry us? It is a poor person who depends upon his moods. If the painter painted only when he was in the mood, he wouldn't get very far. In religion, just as in art and science, besides the time of high inspiration, there are the necessary times of hard work and discipline.

Communication with God must be practiced, otherwise when he surprises us, we are unable to find the right word, the right language, the right tone. We must learn God's language, learn it the hard way with much work, so that we are able to speak to him. Even prayer must be practiced, and with great earnestness.

It is a great and disastrous error to confuse religion with sentimental feelings. Religion is work. And perhaps the hardest and certainly the holiest work that a person can undertake.

What then should we do to experience this rest of our soul in God? I can give you only a brief indication of some of the things we must do. There is not one of us who lives so hectic a life that he cannot spare ten minutes a day—morning or evening—letting himself be still and quieting all around him. Let eternity alone be in your thoughts and in its light question yourself. It can help if there is a verse from the Bible at hand, but best of all, let the mind go free and the soul find its way into the Father's house, returning home to find rest. If anyone works at this, day by day, there will be golden fruits of those times.

Of course, all beginnings are difficult. One may undertake this and at the start find it quite empty. But it does not stay like that. Persist and before long the soul awakes and begins to gain strength. Then comes the eternal rest, which is found in the love of God. Then the troubles and distresses are silenced, the unrest and the hatred, the alarms and the cries, tears and anxieties—all are stilled in the presence of God: "My soul finds rest in God alone; my salvation comes from him."

It is a law of the world that it cannot give rest and peace. Only in God is there stillness and rest. Augustine, the great church father, found the right words for this: "You have created us for yourself, and our hearts are restless until they rest in you."[2]

Harvest Festival Sermon

Berlin, October 4, 1931

Psalm 63

BONHOEFFER WAS ACTIVELY ENGAGED IN LECTURING, church work, and the youth section of the ecumenical movement. Several careers opened up before him: an academic theologian at a time when Berlin had a thousand theological students at its university, an international figure in the ecumenical movement, a churchman who was rapidly gaining experience of church work.

Then something happened to him that might be called a "conversion." He wrote later of turning away from "phraseology to reality"; Bethge titles this section of his biography, "The Theologian Becomes a Christian." A student recalled a conversation in which Bonhoeffer said "that we should not forget that every word of Holy Scripture was a quite personal message of God's love for us," and the student added, "He asked us whether we loved Jesus."

Bonhoeffer was not yet ordained because of his youth, but he was preaching. A month before his ordination in November 1931, he preached a sermon on the evening of October 4 at a harvest festival. His text was Psalm 63.

PSALM 63

O God, you are my God,
  earnestly I seek you;
my soul thirsts for you,
  my body longs for you,
in a dry and weary land
  where there is no water.

I have seen you in the sanctuary
  and beheld your power and your glory.
Because your love is better than life,
  my lips will glorify you.
I will praise you as long as I live,
  and in your name I will lift up my hands.
My soul will be satisfied as with the richest of foods;
  with singing lips my mouth will praise you.

On my bed I remember you;
  I think of you through the watches of the night.
Because you are my help,
  I sing in the shadow of your wings.
My soul clings to you;
  your right hand upholds me.

They who seek my life will be destroyed;
  they will go down to the depths of the earth.
They will be given over to the sword
  and become food for jackals.
But the king will rejoice in God;
  all who swear by God's name will praise him,
  while the mouths of liars will be silenced.

Harvest Festival Sermon

Two and a half millennia ago, a godly Jew, far from home, among mockers and enemies of his God, ponders the wonderful ways in which God has dealt with him. It is not a restful meditation but a struggle, a struggle on the verge of doubt; about life and its meaning, about God and his faithfulness. All that supports life has become fragile. When he reaches out his hand to find support, there is an emptiness. Where are you, God? Where are you? My life falls apart; there is no ground beneath my feet. God has become a worry to me. Where does your love remain? And yet, you are my God and "your love is better than my life."

That is a word that, once you grasp it, never leaves you. It is a word that only appears to be so mild and gentle, but within, it is hard and bursts into flames. It is a passionate word, which is generated where two worlds clash: the world of men and the world of God: that means a word out of the Bible and not from us. "Your love is better than life": that is the triumph cry of the poor and forsaken, the sorrowful and the heavy-laden; the longing cry of the sick and the oppressed; the song of praise by the unemployed and the hungry in our great cities; the song of thanks by the tax collectors and the prostitutes in their public and private sins.

Is that really true? No it is not, at least not in our world, in our time. It is so in the wonderful world of the Bible, whose total strangeness once again annoys and frightens us. That is if we listen to it all and do not become completely deaf to its reality. Or perhaps the Word does not seem so wonderful to us after all? Do we perhaps think that it is all so obvious, and we can learn nothing new from it? Very well, let us see what this psalmist has to say and whether it really has anything to teach us about ourselves.

In the life of our psalmist something decisive happened. It was that God himself came into his life. And from that moment his life was completely changed. I don't mean that from that moment he became good and pious—perhaps he was that already before this happened. But now God himself had come and gone up to him. And now, what made his life so special was that God was always there and he could never be separated from him. God tore his life apart.

We hear and often say that religion makes us happy and contented, peaceful and satisfied. Maybe that is true of religion. For God himself, the living God, that is not so, but basically false. And so it would appear in the life of our psalmist. Something in him has been torn out. He feels himself inwardly split. A struggle burns within him, which from day to day becomes hotter and fiercer. And his experience is that hour by hour what is torn from him is what he loved. He struggles, therefore, because he wants to hold on to it.

But God, who will not let him go, rings him about and he is never free. And the more he loses, the faster he clings to what remains. But God clings yet faster and will not let him go. And so the contest goes on in breathless cycles. God triumphs and the man succumbs. He does not know where it will all lead. He sees himself as lost. He knows not whether to love or to hate the one who has so violently overcome him and destroyed his peace. He fights every inch of the way, but is helpless against the weapons of God.

And it would not be so hopeless for him if these weapons were not so wonderful and special, that they strike him down and raise him up, they wound and yet heal, they kill and make alive. God speaks: Will you let my grace conquer you? Will you let my love hate and destroy the evil in you? Will you let my love take your life?

And now it goes to the limit. All is gone, only one thing remains to the man. And that he would hold fast—his life. But God cannot stop, he launches his assault on this last stronghold. And the battle rages on to the limit. The man is terrified. God cannot wish that. He cannot want to take everything from me. He is not cruel. God is kind. And back comes the answer: If you want my love then surrender the last thing, your life. Choose!

We faint before such conflicts. It is as though we were at the edge of the world. But let me take a homely example. There are two people in love. One says to the other,

"Tell me how much you love me, how much my love is worth to you."

The other replies, "For your love I would give up all I possess."

"Is that all?"

"For your love I would sacrifice my reputation and my honor."

"Is that the limit?"

"For your love I would leave my family and my friends. O if only I could have you. For your love I would give all, all, all."

"Also the very last thing which you still have?"

"You mean would I give up my life for your love? What an impossible contradiction. How can I enjoy your love without my life? Do not ask that of me—and yet, your love is more, is better, than my life."

Who would hesitate to admire with reverence the greatness and strength of such words? Who would not be proud that men are capable of such words?

But how different we Christians are in our love for God. How is it that human passion can sacrifice so much for the beloved and so little when it is a question of God's love? Look how the lover throws away his possessions, his happiness, his honor, his life, gladly for his beloved and seeks ever new sacrifices to make for his love. No price is too high—and now look and see how miserably poor our thanks for the love of God is in comparison!

We think that we have done enough for God's love when we put a few coins in the collection box and maintain a friendly and peaceable attitude.

Why is it so deadly and dreary with us and so lively with those others? Why does the fire that burns so brightly at the beginning become dull with us? Is that the Christian life? Has the life of Christ been portrayed before our eyes like that?

O God, because we no longer know you, because we no longer seek you, because we no longer understand how awful it is to live without thinking about you, that you are the beginning and the end of our life and our judge in eternity! Because we no longer see the love of God in the life of Jesus Christ and let it rouse us to new life. Because we cling to ourselves and wish to stand by ourselves. Because we cannot believe that God alone can lead us aright and give eternal meaning to our life even when it is outwardly shattered. But that is because we have sinned against God's incomparable honor and love and have become guilty before him.

God holds us responsible and we refuse to accept it because we depend still more upon ourselves and trust ourselves rather than God. God asks us how much we value his love and we answer: in any case, less than we value our own. So we push God's love out of our lives.

But now there occurs the greatest miracle that the world has ever known. There, where we have fallen away from God, where we are dead to God and unresponsive in our guilt, there the love of God seeks us out and reveals itself anew as the eternal promise of God in Jesus Christ. Only the one who knows the love of God, who has been deep in the darkness of faithlessness and enmity to God, feels the disturbing power of love, which never ceases, which forgives all and who from all distress comes into God's world.

There is no relief from this assault upon our life. We cannot escape our responsibility and ever anew God asks: What is my love worth? The more profoundly we recognize what the love of God is, the more lively will our answer be. Again and again we are led by God's love into responsibility, through our very guilt, to him.

When will the world of our psalmist break into at least the Christian community, so that we, whether in joy or in sorrow, in hunger, in sickness, in fear and trouble, in sadness and deepest guilt, in good and bad harvests, can say with triumph: "And though they take our life, goods, honor, children, wife, yet is their profit small; these things shall vanish all, the city of God remains."

"God, your love is better than life." Amen.[3]

Morning Address during an Ecumenical Conference

Fanö, Denmark,
August 28, 1934

Psalm 85

THE YEAR 1933 WAS A DANGEROUS ONE FOR BONHOEFFER. A few days after Hitler's rise to power, Bonhoeffer was broadcasting on the dangers of the "leadership principle," a concept central to the Nazi doctrine. Shortly afterwards he circulated a document on "The Jewish Problem" that severely criticized the use the Nazis were making of Martin Luther in their campaign against the Jews. In the same year, Bonhoeffer helped draft a statement of faith for the Confessing Church, which included a sharp attack on the Nazi treatment of the Jews. Later, that paragraph was not accepted in the final version of the "Barmen Declaration."

Bonhoeffer was becoming disillusioned with the Confessing Church, and he himself was very much a marked man.

In October 1933, he went to London to become pastor of two German-speaking congregations there. While in England he worked closely with George Bell, bishop of Chichester and chairman of the World Alliance (later to become the World Council of Churches). His main concern was what was happening in Germany, and he kept Bishop Bell well informed. Bonhoeffer also became more and more involved in the ecumenical movement. He supported Bishop Bell in his effort to put the weight of the World Church behind the efforts of the Confessing Church in Germany to keep the church free from Nazi control.

Although Bonhoeffer was in England when the First Synod of the Confessing Church was held in Barmen, Germany, at the end of May 1934, he nevertheless followed it closely and enabled the bishop of Chichester to convey its importance to the British public in the House of Lords and the *Times* newspaper.

In August, Bonhoeffer attended the meeting of the World Alliance, Universal Christian Council in Fanö, Denmark, where he was invited to speak. He took as his theme "The Church and the Peoples of the World." He delivered the address in English and based his message upon Psalm 85, concentrating upon verse 8 of the King James Version: "I will hear what God the LORD will speak: for he will speak peace unto his people, and to his saints."

PSALM 85

You showed favor to your land, O LORD;
*   you restored the fortunes of Jacob.*
You forgave the iniquity of your people
*   and covered all their sins.*   Selah
You set aside all your wrath
*   and turned from your fierce anger.*

Restore us again, O God our Savior,
*   and put away your displeasure toward us.*

Will you be angry with us forever?
  Will you prolong your anger through all
  generations?
Will you not revive us again,
  that your people may rejoice in you?
Show us your unfailing love, O LORD,
  and grant us your salvation.

I will listen to what God the LORD will say;
  he promises peace to his people, his saints—
  but let them not return to folly.
Surely his salvation is near those who fear him,
  that his glory may dwell in our land.

Love and faithfulness meet together;
  righteousness and peace kiss each other.
Faithfulness springs forth from the earth,
  and righteousness looks down from heaven.
The LORD will indeed give what is good,
  and our land will yield its harvest.
Righteousness goes before him
  and prepares the way for his steps.

Morning Address during an Ecumenical Conference

I will hear what God the LORD will speak:
for he will speak peace unto his people,
and to his saints.

Psalm 85:8 KJV

Between the twin crags of nationalism and internationalism, ecumenical Christendom calls upon her Lord and asks his guidance. Nationalism and internationalism have to do with political necessities and possibilities. The ecumenical church, however, does not concern itself with these things but with the commandments of God, and regardless of consequences, it transmits these commandments to the world.

Our task as theologians, accordingly, consists only in accepting the commandment as a binding one, not as a question open to discussion. Peace on earth is not a problem but a commandment given at Christ's coming.

There are two ways of reacting to this command from God: the unconditional, blind obedience of action, or the hypocritical question of the Serpent, "Yea, hath God said . . . ?" This question is the mortal enemy of obedience and, therefore, the mortal enemy of all real peace. "Hath God not said? Has God not understood human nature well enough to know that wars must occur in this world, like laws of nature? Must God not have meant that we should talk about peace, to be sure, but that it is not to be literally translated into action? Must God not really have said that we should work for peace but also make ready tanks and poison gas for security?" And then perhaps the most serious question, "Did God say that you should not protect your own people? Did God say you should leave your own a prey to the enemy?"

No, God did not say all that. What he has said is that there should be peace among men—that we shall obey him without further question, that is what he means. He who questions the commandments of God before obeying has already denied him.

There shall be peace because of the church of Christ, for the sake of which the world exists. And this church of Christ lives at one and the same time in all peoples, beyond all boundaries, whether national, political, social, or racial. And the brothers who make up this church are bound together, through the commandment of the one Lord Christ, whose word they hear, more inseparably than men are bound by all the ties of common history, of blood, of class, and of language. All these ties, which are part of our world, are valid ties, not indifferent: but in the presence of Christ they are not ultimate bonds.

For the members of the ecumenical church, insofar as they hold to Christ, his word, his commandment of peace is more holy, more inviolable than the most revered words and works of the natural world. For they know that whosoever is not able to hate father and mother for his sake is not worthy of him, and lies if he calls himself after Christ's name. These brothers in Christ obey his word; they do not doubt or question, but keep his commandment of peace. They are not ashamed, in defiance of the world, even to speak of eternal peace. They cannot take up arms against Christ himself—yet this is what they do if they take up arms against one another! Even in anguish and distress of conscience there is for them no escape from the commandment of Christ that there shall be peace.

How does peace come about? Through a system of political treaties? Through the investment of international capital in different countries? Through the big banks, through money? Or through universal peaceful rearmament to guarantee peace? Through none of these, for the single reason of them all, peace is confused with safety. There is no way to peace along the way of safety. For peace must be dared. It is the great venture. It can never be safe. Peace is the opposite of security. To demand guarantees is to mistrust, and this mistrust in turn brings forth war. To look for guarantees is to want to protect oneself.

Peace means to give oneself altogether to the law of God, wanting no security, but in faith and obedience laying the destiny of the nations in the hand of the almighty God, not trying to direct it for selfish purposes. Battles are won, not with weapons, but with God. They are won where the way leads to the Cross. Which of us can say he knows what it might mean for the world if one nation should meet the aggressor, not with weapons in hand, but praying, defenseless, and for that very reason protected by "a bulwark never failing"?

Once again, how will peace come? Who will call us to peace so that the world will hear, will have to hear, so that all peoples may rejoice? The individual Christian cannot do it. When all around are silent, he can indeed raise his voice and bear witness, but the powers of the world stride over him without a word. The individual too can witness and suffer—oh, if he only would—but he also is suffocated by the power of hate.

Only the one great Ecumenical Council of the holy church of Christ over all the world can speak out so that the world, though it gnash its teeth, will have to hear, so that the peoples will rejoice because the church of Christ in the name of Christ has taken the weapons from the hands of their sons, forbidden war, proclaimed the peace of Christ against the raging world.

Why do we fear the fury of the world powers? Why don't we take the power from them and give it back to Christ? We can still do it today. The Ecumenical Council is in session; it can send out to all believers the radical call to peace. The nations are waiting for it in the East and in the West. Must we be put to shame by non-

Christian people in the East? Shall we desert the individuals who are risking their lives for this message?

The hour is late. The world is choked with weapons, and dreadful is the mistrust that looks out of all men's eyes. The trumpets of war may blow tomorrow. For what are we waiting? Do we want to become involved in this guilt as never before?

> *What use to me are crown, land, folk and fame?*
> *They cannot cheer my breast!*
> *War's in the land, alas, and on my name*
> *I pray no guilt may rest.*
>
> Mattheus Claudius

We want to give the world a whole word, not a half word—a courageous word, a Christian word. We want to pray that this word may be given us today. Who knows if we shall see each other again another year?[4]

Sermon on God's Righteous Anger

Finkenwalde, July 11, 1937

Psalm 58

WHILE BONHOEFFER WAS IN HIS LONDON PASTORATE, he asked the bishop of Chichester to write a letter of recommendation to Mahatma Gandhi, whom he had long wished to visit. Before he could make this visit, however, an urgent invitation came from the Confessing Church of the Old Prussian Union, calling him back to Germany to direct a pastors' seminary. Before leaving, he visited, as a substitute for Gandhi, three monastic centers of the Church of England—Kelham, Mirfield, and the Oxford Fathers. He also visited various theological seminaries of other denominations, such as the Methodist one at Richmond.

But it was Mirfield which most affected his reading of the Psalms. There, the Community of the Resurrection went through the long Psalm 119 each day of his visit, praying their way through it. It was this experience which led to his fascination with that psalm, which from then on he referred to more than any other.

The other effect was to change his way of interpreting the Psalms. As earlier examples show, he had had a tendency to concentrate upon one or maybe two verses as his text. While of course he took seriously the context, he emphasized the relevance of these chosen verses. In the frantic rebuilding of Berlin, for example, he concentrated on "Unless the LORD builds the house, its builders labor in vain." When he returned to his teaching at the Old Prussian Union Confessing Church Seminary, he began to look at psalms as a whole. He also transported into the seminary, which eventually settled at Finkenwalde, the ideas of confession and community life.

Bonhoeffer met his first students at Zingshof on the Baltic on April 26, 1935. The accommodation there was primitive and inadequate, so the seminary was moved to Finkenwalde, a small town near Stettin. Bonhoeffer was happy to be back and teaching. In the autumn of 1935 he wrote to one of his students, "The summer of 1935 has been the fullest time of my life, both from the professional and human point of view."

He helped train a group of pastors who would keep the truth in trying times, and indeed many suffered for their faith. Gradually the seminary became involved in the struggle of the Confessing Church to keep the church independent of the state. The Nazi government increased its pressure and severe measures were taken. Martin Niemöller was arrested in 1937 and remained in prison until 1945. The seminary was closed by the Gestapo in the same year, but Bonhoeffer continued in a clandestine way to direct the work in scattered parishes of Pomerania.

In this situation, he expounded a savage psalm of revenge.

PSALM 58

Do you rulers indeed speak justly?
  Do you judge uprightly among men?
No, in your heart you devise injustice,
  and your hands mete out violence on the earth.
Even from birth the wicked go astray;
  from the womb they are wayward and speak lies.

Their venom is like the venom of a snake,
  like that of a cobra that has stopped its ears,
that will not heed the tune of the enchanter,
  however skillful the enchanter may be.

Break the teeth in their mouths, O God;
  tear out, O LORD, the fangs of the lions!
Let them vanish like water that flows away;
  when they draw the bow, let their arrows be
  blunted.
Like a slug melting away as it moves along,
  like a stillborn child, may they not see the sun.

Before your pots can feel the heat of the thorns—
  whether they be green or dry—the wicked will be
  swept away.
The righteous will be glad when they are avenged,
  when they bathe their feet in the blood of the
  wicked.
Then men will say,
  "Surely the righteous still are rewarded;
  surely there is a God who judges the earth."

Sermon on
God's Righteous Anger

Can this awful psalm of anger really be our prayer? Dare we pray in such a manner? The answer is perfectly clear—No! We cannot pray this psalm.

Despite all the hostility against us and all the trouble into which our enemies lead us, we are too conscious of our own guilt. God is just to strike a man down in his sinfulness. But we know even in these troubled times for the church, that God may justly raise his arm in anger against us too. If he does, it is to make us recognize our sins, our spiritual lethargy, our private and our public disobediences, and the lack of discipline in our daily life. All these are under the judgment of God.

How can we deny that our personal sins, even those which we think to hide, bring down God's wrath upon his church? What right then have we, we who are ourselves guilty and deserving of God's wrath, to call for his vengeance against our enemies, without expecting this same wrath to be called down upon us? No, we cannot pray this psalm. Not because we are much too good to do that—what a superficial thought, what inconceivable arrogance—but because we are too sinful, too bad to do that.

Only one who is without guilt can pray this psalm. The psalm of vengeance is the prayer of the innocent.

The psalm is described as "A psalm of David, set to the music of 'Do not destroy.'" It is David who prays this psalm. David himself is not innocent.

But God has chosen to prepare in David one who will be called the Son of David, Jesus Christ. Therefore David must not be destroyed, because through him shall come the Christ. David could never have prayed that his own life should be preserved from his enemies. We know that David personally committed many sinful acts. But in David is the Christ, and with him the church of God. Therefore his enemies are the enemies of Jesus Christ and of his holy church. For this reason, David must not be destroyed by his enemies. Thus in David, the innocence of Christ prays this psalm, and with Christ, the whole holy church.

No, we sinners cannot pray this song of vengeance, but the only one without sin may pray it. The sinless Christ stands before the world and accuses it. We cannot accuse, Christ accuses. And when Christ charges the world with sin, we are soon to be found among the defendants.

> *Do you rulers indeed speak justly?*
> *Do you judge uprightly among men? No.*
> *(vv. 1–2)*

Luther's translation has "Are you dumb, that you do not speak justly?" It is an evil time when the world is dumb before injustice. When the oppressed, the poor, the deprived, cry aloud unto heaven, while the judges and the lords of the earth keep silent. When the persecuted church calls upon God for help and upon men for justice, while no one on earth speaks to give what is right: "Are you dumb, that you do not speak justly, and judge the children of men uprightly?" It is the children of men who are treated unjustly. Must that be forgotten in such times as these?

Listen: children of men, creatures of God, like you, who feel pain and sorrow like you, to whom violence is done; who have joys and hopes like you; who feel honor and insult like you; children of men, who are sinners like you and who seek God's compassion as we do: your brothers! "Are you dumb?" O no, you are not dumb, your voice is heard, loud and clear on earth! But the words you speak are not compassionate; they are the words of your party. They are not intended to judge uprightly but to please those in power.

No, in your heart you devise injustice,
and your hands mete out violence on the earth.
(v. 2)

When the rulers are silent before injustice, then the evil hand of violence is not far off. The violent language of human hands is fearful when there is no justice. Thereby comes trouble and pain of body, one sees the persecuted, the imprisoned, the smitten, church, which longs to be released from this body. "Let us fall into the hands of the LORD ... but do not let me fall into the hands of men" (2 Samuel 24:14). Do we still hear it? Christ speaks here! He experienced the unjust judgment, he fell into the hands of men. The guiltless one accuses the unjust world. As sinners we come up against only the just anger of God.

But it cannot be otherwise. It is not a matter of a few isolated failures. No. Here the secret of godlessness itself is revealed.

Even from birth the wicked go astray;
from the womb they are wayward and speak lies.
(v. 3)

Only the sinless one can see the depth of this evil. We would like to believe that it is still possible to change, to improve, and we seek all kinds of ways to achieve this. But we get nowhere, except more disappointment, indignant and disturbed as ever more weighty injustice follows. The sinless one alone knows that everything must go on as it is. The sinless one knows that Satan is already at work in the mother's womb and drives on rapidly. Now they must do his work. World is world, Satan is Satan. In this background of knowledge, the sinless one is at the same time at peace. It must be so and it will not change.

Their venom is like the venom of a snake,
like that of a cobra that has stopped its ears,

that will not heed the tune of the charmer,
however skillful the enchanter may be. (vv. 4–5)

Eastern countries are familiar with the snake charmer, whose snakes with their tongues tamed must always be obedient. But the deaf snake does not hear the voice of the charmer and cares nothing for him.

God himself is the charmer who can charm wonderfully. It is with his word of grace that he bewitches and charms our hearts. He lures us with the sweet words of his love, he overcomes us, he conquers our heart, so that we, as though we had been hypnotized, hear him and must be obedient to him.

But there remains the great mystery that some should hear and some have deaf ears, so that they are stopped from hearing. We know from our own experience that there are times when our ears are deaf. These are times when in conscious disobedience we set our heart against God's will, and sin adds to sin, until finally we hear no more, then Satan becomes our master. Satan so hardens our heart that we must obey him in his struggle against God's kingdom and his words. These you can no longer hear, no longer obey. Because your ear is deaf to the grace of God, your mouth is dumb and unable to speak out for the justice of God. These are the enemies of God and his church, as David, as Christ, as the church recognizes.

This knowledge leads to prayer. When this is the enemy, no human arts can help to attain peace. Then no human power helps any more to overcome this enemy. God's name must be called upon. And now, in our psalm, that terrible prayer that begins, which we dread, which we repeat only with trembling and deep inner resistance, when we read it. God will be called upon to execute vengeance on the enemy.

> *Break the teeth in their mouths, O God;*
> *tear out, O LORD, the fangs of the lions! (v. 6)*

Here, above all, we must learn this: faced with the enemy of God and his church, we can only pray. Our courage, be it ever so great, all our steadfastness before this enemy is shattered to pieces. It is with the onslaught of Satan that we have to do. This matter has to be put into the hands that alone are stronger than Satan, God himself. It will be much if we have learnt this, that we must earnestly pray to God in such dire distress.

Now David breaks out into an immeasurable jubilation. He is quite sure that his prayer has been heard. In rapid images he portrays the distress and suffering of the godless, seen as already defeated while the battle rages.

> *Let them vanish like water that flows away. (v. 7)*

Quickly and suddenly will be their end. As water disappears quickly, so they will no longer be there:

> *When they draw the bow, let their arrows be blunted.*
> *(v. 7)*

Their deadly arrows still whiz through the air, but they can do no harm, they are powerless.

> *Like a slug melting away as it moves along. (v. 8)*

So full of contempt for his enemy, David now describes him as a slug!

David now speaks of his enemies with contempt. As one treads upon a slug, so will it be when God will tread underfoot the powerful and great "lords of the earth."

like a stillborn child, may they not see the sun. (v. 8)

They shall be quickly disposed of. They will remain in darkness and forgotten, and no one will inquire of them.

Before your pots can feel the heat of the thorns—
whether they be green or dry—the wicked will be
swept away. (v. 9)

God's anger will not give the enemy time to ripen their plans. Before then, the godless will be swept away with violence. They finalize nothing—that is God's revenge. It will come quickly, quicker than we expect!

The righteous will be glad when they are avenged,
when they bathe their feet in the blood of the
wicked. (v. 10)

Once more we avert our eyes from this psalm. Is it not quite impossible for us Christians to pray for such an end? Dear congregation, once again we want to turn away from this psalm we have not fully understood. This verse and this whole psalm is about God and his righteousness. The godless must die and thereby God's righteousness triumphs. In this verse we are no longer concerned with human friendliness and human compassion, but only that God is seen to triumph.

Whoever shrinks with horror at this joy over the vengeance of God and the blood of the godless does not yet know what happens at the cross of Christ. God's righteous vengeance over the godless has already become clear to us. The blood of the godless has already poured out. God's judgment of death over the godless has already been spoken. God's righteousness is fulfilled. That has happened in the cross of Jesus Christ.

Jesus Christ died, under God's anger and vengeance, the death of the godless. His blood is the blood God demanded for the breaking of the commandments. God's revenge is executed, more than the psalm itself knows, "on earth." Christ, the sinless, died the death of the godless, that we should not have to die. Now we stand, as the godless, under his cross and now a mystery, hard to comprehend, is resolved: in the hour of God's vengeance on the godless on earth, the sinless one prays that our psalm might be fulfilled: "Father, forgive them for they know not what they do" (Luke 23:34 KJV).

Only he who bore the anger of God, only he may ask forgiveness for the godless. Thus he alone has made us free from God's anger and vengeance, he has brought forgiveness to his enemies and none of them are able so to pray. He alone can do it. When we behold him, the crucified, we understand God's just and living anger against us godless, and at the same time, the liberation from his anger, as we hear:

> *Father, forgive them; for they know not what they do.*
>
> Luke 23:34 KJV

> *The righteous will be glad when they are avenged,*
>   *when they bathe their feet in the blood of the*
>   *wicked.*
>
> Psalm 58:10

Is that not truly God's joy? Is that not joy of the righteous that God's righteousness has triumphed on the cross, joy over the victory of Christ? God's anger is extinguished, and the blood of the godless, in which we bathe our feet, gives to us a part in the victory of God. The blood of the godless has become our redemption; it cleanses us from sin. That is the miracle.

> *Then men will say, "Surely the righteous still are*
>   *rewarded." (v. 11)*

Luther's translation has, "Surely the righteous will yet bear fruit."

The fruit of righteousness is not happiness nor power nor the honors of this world. It is none other than the fellowship of the cross of Jesus Christ, that satisfaction of the anger of God.

> *"Surely there is a God who judges the earth." (v. 11)*

Where then is God's judgment over the godless of the earth? Not in obvious sorrow, failure, and shame before the world, but only in the cross of Jesus Christ. Is that not enough for us? What more should all our suffering wish than this judgment of God? And so, when we are dissatisfied with God's judgment on earth, let us look upon the cross of Christ: here is judgment, here is pardon.

What we cannot see until the Last Judgment—the deliverance of the righteous and the condemnation of the godless—is hidden from us by the love of the crucified. We cannot bear this on earth. But we can be sure of this, that all will serve the joy of the righteous. But until that last day, Satan will continue to fight against the Christ and his church, with injustice, violence, and lies. In the midst of this fury, Christ prays this psalm for us. He condemns the godless, he calls for God's anger and justice upon them and he gives himself, also for the godless, by his sinless suffering on the cross.

And now we may pray this psalm with him, in humble thanks that by the cross of Christ, we are delivered from the anger and the justice of God.[5]

Meditations
from the *Losungen*

Pomerania, Christmas 1937

*Psalms 41; 104;
25; 20; 71*

AFTER THE CLOSING OF THE SEMINARY AT FINKENWALDE in
September 1937, Bonhoeffer went home to Berlin. He
now had more time with the family and with his brother-
in-law, Hans von Dohnanyi, who was deeply involved in
a resistance movement against the Nazi regime. Up to
this point, Bonhoeffer had kept his protests within the
law; he had defended the churches' rights. Even his
protest against the treatment of the Jews was at its
strongest when he defended the right of the church to
select its own pastors, without interference from the
state. Now he was tempted into political activity.

Life in Berlin was very pleasant, but Bonhoeffer did
not give up his training of students from the Confessing
Church. He and his friend Eberhard Bethge worked at
assigning each student to a sympathetic incumbent as an
assistant. They were to be ministers in training and Bonhoeffer and Bethge, now director of studies, traveled
throughout the province. They obtained two centers and
divided the students into two groups. Work then continued as at Finkenwalde but less comfortably and illegally.

Apart from his visits, Bonhoeffer wrote circular letters. He could not publish, nor was he allowed to preach
or hold assembly. He, like so many Germans at that
time—and to a certain extent still—used the daily
Losungen. Every year this book is prepared by the Mora-
vians for daily devotion. The title means "lozenges"—to

be taken daily! Each day has a series of Bible passages to read and a verse of a hymn.

It was Bonhoeffer's custom to comment on these verses and from time to time to circulate his comments. He did this at the end of 1937. Of the eight days at the end of the year, from Christmas Eve to the last day of the year, Silvester Day, five of them included verses from the Psalms. His comments are very personal and show how much the Psalms helped him to maintain his relationship with God.

That year, 1937, had raised questions about his role as a Lutheran minister and caused him deep anxiety about his faith. The loss of his seminary at Finkenwalde had left him more or less unemployed. He suffered no great hardships and even felt guilty at the comfort of life in Berlin. Soon he would have to make crucial decisions about his future.

Early in 1938 he was introduced by his brother-in-law to the four leading conspirators in the Department of Military Intelligence (the Abwehr). He was not yet ready to join them. Soon his call-up for military service would present him with a major decision. But that was not until 1939.

Although happy with his family in Berlin, enjoying music, meals, leisure, and a warm social life, he listened to the psalmist.

Christmas Eve:

The Manger as the
Place for a Confession

PSALM 41:4–5

I said, "O LORD, have mercy on me;
heal me, for I have sinned against you."
My enemies say of me in malice,
"When will he die and his name perish?"

This is a confession. The manger, where the Son of God came in the flesh, is the right place for our confession. The One who assumed our flesh and blood knows our heart. We are all damaged and torn by our manifold sins. Where else should we seek grace for all our unfaithfulness, all our little faith, all our betrayal, than the manger where God humbled himself? Where else would we seek healing for our soul, for our life, than with him who appears to us as Savior?

No one would wish to go into these Christmas days without finding the time, despite all our work and restlessness, to lay down our confessions before our Lord Jesus. Then he would share with us his humility and innocence.

To the one who is alone and lacking brotherly companionship and support, God reveals in a wonderful way true companionship, wherever we are. We speak then in the spirit that so often comes upon as at the Table of the Lord: Heal my soul; for I have sinned against thee. So shall we be thankful, on this Holy Night, once more for the grace of God.

December 26:

God's World Is Full of Fruits

PSALM 104:13–14

He waters the mountains from his upper chambers;
the earth is satisfied by the fruit of his work.
He makes grass grow for the cattle,
and plants for man to cultivate—
bringing forth food from the earth.

The One who has sent us the Savior will also care for our physical well-being, as long as we are on this earth. It is his world. It must serve his purposes. The Father will give to his beloved children in Christ what they need.

The one who has set his faith in Christ need not worry about the morrow. In the midst of the coldest winter, we should see God's earth already full of fruitfulness. Should that be too difficult for us, we who saw in the darkest night the eternal light shining? We who have seen the tiny flower spring up in the night of winter? "Es ist ein Ros' entsprochen" ["Lo How a Rose E'er Blooming," the familiar carol by Schubert about the tiny rose blooming in winter]. By the power and the love of God, the heavenly spring is already breaking—". . . mitten im kalten winter wohl zu der halben Nacht" ["a rose has bloomed in the cold winter, even in the twilight"].

December 29:
The Birth of Christ

PSALM 25:10

*All the ways of the LORD are loving and faithful
for those who keep the demands of his covenant.*

Can you, after you have experienced this hard year, still say today, "All the ways of the LORD are loving and faithful"? Did you know that God was good to you when he sent distress and imprisonment? Can you recognize God as the true and faithful one when he has taken so much away from you?

No one can say yes to God's ways who has said no to his promises and commandments. Acceptance of the will of God comes in the daily submission under his Word. It may be to us only a slight disobedience, and yet it takes from us that thanks and praise for God's ways that come from the heart. To come under the yoke of Christ is painful and hard if we do it against our will. It is easy and gentle when God has won and conquered the heart at Christmastime.

December 30:

Unfurling the Banners

PSALM 20:5

We will shout for joy when you are victorious
and will lift up our banners in the name of our God.

In recent times of great distress for the church, there have been many offers of human help. Even when they have been well meant, they have only brought temptations upon us. How then shall the best human will of the church help us in our struggle with the Devil?

We have celebrated Christmas. Jesus is born. He is our helper. He alone. Here is God's help for people in temptation and distress. Is this help not enough? Are we becoming impatient?

Let us meet all temptations with the joyful confession: We will shout for joy that he helps us. We will unfurl our banners in the struggle. By you stands Jesus the helper.

December 31:

Throughout the Years Proclaim His Might

PSALM 71:18

Even when I am old and gray,
do not forsake me, O God,

till I declare your power to the next generation,
  your might to all who are to come.

With amazement we stand at the end of another year. For a long time now, we have grown used to not reckoning with long periods of time. We cannot, neither should we, do this. Learning to be obedient each new day is enough for us.

But time marches on and our text for today speaks to us of growing old. It is, despite everything, right this once to fix our eyes upon the fact that we may have a long life in front of us: that the last day may not come tomorrow or the day after. "For this is what the LORD Almighty, the God of Israel, says: Houses, fields and vineyards will again be bought in this land" (Jeremiah 32:15). Perhaps we shall grow gray in this church struggle and new generations bear new burdens upon their shoulders.

Therefore, we pray God, before whom a thousand years is like a day, for the grace that will allow us to proclaim his might through the years. Years and generations pass, but the Word of God does not pass. We are only a link in the chain.

Yet the anxious and joyful question remains: Which generation will experience the Last Day? Amen, come quickly, Lord Jesus![6]

Kristallnacht (Crystal Night)

November 9, 1938

Psalm 74

BONHOEFFER WAS ALREADY LOSING PATIENCE with the Confessing Church because of its reluctance to condemn the persecution of the Jews. The crisis came on the night of November 9, 1938, when the Nazi thugs were allowed, unhindered by the police, to do what they wanted with Jews and Jewish property. The occasion was the attempted assassination of the German ambassador in Paris by a deranged Polish Jew. He failed, but it gave the Nazis their excuse to ill-treat and even murder Jews. They broke into Jewish shops and destroyed or stole anything they liked. The broken glass that littered the streets gave that awful night the elegant name of *Kristallnacht* (Crystal Night). Among other desecrations were the burning of synagogues.

It was not until two days later that Bonhoeffer first met the full violence of *Kristallnacht*. He went to Köslin (Pomerania) and saw the smoldering ruins of the synagogue there; the same sight in Stettin; and the desecration of the Jewish cemetery in Schlawe. All these places were where he had worked with his students, and the destruction appalled him. There is little doubt that these sights strengthened his decision to join the Conspiracy and destroy this monstrous tyranny. He was not allowed to preach, but he turned to his Bible and read Psalm 74. He had been preparing preaching notes for his Finkenwalde students, now scattered throughout Pomerania. He added to his notes the advice that they should read:

Psalm 74; Zechariah 2:8; Romans 9:4; and 11:11–15.
He urged his students to read these passages and take
heed to the words: "Whoever touches you touches the
apple of his eye" (Zechariah 2:8). Bonhoeffer himself
marked Psalm 74 in his Bible with the date 9-11-38.

PSALM 74:1–11

Why have you rejected us forever, O God?
   Why does your anger smolder against the sheep
      of your pasture?
Remember the people you purchased of old,
   the tribe of your inheritance, whom you redeemed—
Mount Zion, where you dwelt.
Turn your steps toward these everlasting ruins,
   all this destruction the enemy has brought on the
      sanctuary.

Your foes roared in the place where you met with us;
   they set up their standards as signs.
They behaved like men wielding axes
   to cut through a thicket of trees.
They smashed all the carved paneling
   with their axes and hatchets.
They burned your sanctuary to the ground;
   they defiled the dwelling place of your Name.
They said in their hearts, "We will crush them
      completely!"

*They burned every place where God was worshiped
    in the land.*
We are given no miraculous signs;
    no prophets are left,
    and none of us knows how long this will be.

How long will the enemy mock you, O God?
    Will the foe revile your name forever?
Why do you hold back your hand, your right hand?
    *Take it from the folds of your garment and destroy
        them!*

Kristallnacht (Crystal Night)

It was probably at this time that Bonhoeffer coined the
saying so often repeated: "Only he who cries out for the
Jews may sing Gregorian chants." In his Bible he under-
lined the second half of verse 8: "They burned every
place where God was worshiped in the land" and brack-
eted the next verse in the margin: "We are given no
miraculous signs; no prophets are left, and none of us
knows how long this will be."

These may be cryptic comments, but they are clear
enough. Bethge comments that, because of the weak
actions of the Confessing Church "in that evil year,"
Bonhoeffer began to separate himself from the rearguard

actions of its defeated remnants. Bonhoeffer saw Psalm 74 as a description of *Kristallnacht,* and he lost faith in the church resistance. Henceforth he was prepared to be politically involved.

With Eyes Wide Open— Meditations

Berlin to New York and Back, 1939–40

Psalm 119

THE YEAR 1939 WAS PROBABLY THE MOST CONFUSED in Bonhoeffer's life. In Germany the political situation became more and more intolerable. The conspirators had great hopes of the Münich Conference when Neville Chamberlain and Daladier (France) met Mussolini and Hitler. The military men whom Bonhoeffer had met in 1938 did not think of themselves as conspirators but as patriots determined to rid Germany of its maniac leader. They expected Hitler to be rebuffed at Münich and had planned a coup. The result shattered them. Hitler had won first Sudetenland, and then the whole of Czechoslovakia was annexed to him. Bonhoeffer was invited to join the resistance, but he was long in deciding. The whole idea of a Lutheran pastor overthrowing the legitimate government of the state was outside his realm of thinking.

After Münich came *Kristallnacht,* November 9, 1938, and the persecution of the Jews seemed total. Bonhoeffer had already helped his twin sister and her Jewish husband escape.

Added to this confusion was the fact that in 1939 Bonhoeffer was due to be drafted for military service; since he could not swear allegiance to his führer, he sought ways of avoiding it. He and his friend Eberhard Bethge went to England to consult with the bishop of Chichester (George Bell) and later Reinhold Niebuhr of the U.S.

Eventually he was invited to America for a lecture tour. As the war clouds gathered over Europe he saw his mistake. If he stayed in America he would not return to Germany until the war—which was by now inevitable—was over. He made his decision to return. Many of his reasons for returning were confusing, but writing to Reinhold Niebuhr, he put it plainly enough:

> Christians in Germany will face the terrible alternative of either willing the defeat of their nation in order that Christian civilization may survive, or willing the victory of their nation and thereby destroying civilization. I know which of these alternatives I must choose but I cannot make the choice in security.

He returned, knowing the dangers, and joined the resistance. He avoided military service by being co-opted to the Abwehr, the military intelligence network that was immune from investigation by the Gestapo and the center of the resistance to Hitler.

During this baffling period, Bonhoeffer directed his attention even more closely to the Psalms. He wrote *Das Gebethbuch der Bibel (The Prayer Book of the Bible)* in which he classified the Psalms under the headings of: "The Creation," "The Law," "The Story of Salvation," "The Messiah," "The Church," "Life," "Suffering," "Guilt," "The Enemy," and "The End."

As he listed the psalms under these headings he discussed their meanings as they related to his own situation, and the "terrible alternative" was never far away. This was the last book he had printed in his lifetime. The very title and introduction explained what he said often to his students: "The only way to read the Psalms is on your knees in prayer."

Throughout this period, the long Psalm 119 absorbed his attention. It fascinated him—its strange structure, each section beginning with a letter of the Hebrew alphabet in turn; and the prayers at Mirfield, where verse by verse they prayed through this great psalm in praise of the Law. His meditations on Psalm 119 are not complete, but what we have is enough to show how he prayed section by section. He gave titles to the twenty-two sections that show the immense range of his interpretation.

The manuscript breaks off after only three of the twenty-two sections, and the third is unfinished.

The first three sections are:

I. Praise vv. 1–4
II. Guiltless vv. 5–16
III. With Eyes Wide Open vv. 17–26

The first is naturally the longest and the second is six or seven pages shorter. How long the third would have been we do not know, but it is the most interesting and its sudden end tantalizing!

III. WITH EYES WIDE OPEN PSALM 119:17–26

Do good to your servant, and I will live;
  I will obey your word.
Open my eyes that I may see

> *wonderful things in your law.*
> *I am a stranger on earth;*
>> *do not hide your commands from me.*
> *My soul is consumed with longing*
>> *for your laws at all times.*
> *You rebuke the arrogant, who are cursed*
>> *and who stray from your commands.*
> *Remove from me scorn and contempt,*
>> *for I keep your statutes.*
> *Though rulers sit together and slander me,*
>> *your servant will meditate on your decrees.*
> *Your statutes are my delight;*
>> *they are my counselors.*

With Eyes Wide Open— Meditations

Do good to your servant, and I will live. (v. 17)

I ask about life as the servant to his master. Life is God's gift. Life is not a means to an end, but it is fulfilled in itself. God created us, therefore we live. He reconciled and redeemed us, therefore we live. He will not see ideas triumph over a killing field of corpses. Ideas are for the sake of life, not life for the sake of ideas. When life itself is made into an idea then the real created and redeemed life is destroyed.

Life is God's purpose for us. When it is only a means
to an end, then a contradiction enters into life leading to
torment. When one seeks the end, the perfection, the
other side of life, it can only be purchased by destroying
life. That is the situation we are in before we receive life
from God, and we are taught to accept this situation as
good! We thus come to hate and despise life as it is and
to be enchanted by ideas.

I ask God about the goodness of life. Only the life that
he gives is good. All other life is torment. Only life from
God is the goal and the fulfillment, overcoming the contradiction between what is and what should be. The time
of life is grace, of death is judgment. Therefore life is divine
goodness because time given to me is by the grace of God.
Such time is available so long as the Word of God is by me.

To hold this Word fast is to affirm life from God.
God's Word is not the other side of earthly life, it does
not degrade such life to become only a means to an end,
but it protects life from the decadence of contradiction
in the realm of ideas. God's Word is the fulfillment of life,
beyond which there is no "end." For this reason I ask
God about the goodness of life, which has befallen me
as the servant of the Lord, and how it will be fulfilled
through holding fast to the Word of God.

Open my eyes that I may see. (v. 18)

I must close the eyes of my senses if I am to see what
God would show me. When he wants me to see his

Word, God makes me blind. He then makes the blind to see. Then I see what otherwise I would never have known, that God's law is full of wonders.

How could I make my long way through this psalm and again and again turn to it anew, how could I not become weary of this constant repetition, if God did not give me to understand that every one of his words is full of unrevealed and undiscovered wonders? How could I, day by day, study God's Word without eyes wide open to see the glory and depth of these words? God's law may perhaps use the eyes of my learning as a necessary preliminary, but very soon all is learned and grasped to give rules for living. There is then not much more thinking, reading, or studying to do.

So long as I am content to use these eyes, I have no longing that my eyes should be open wide. When I was blind, God led me into the deepest night, put me into the darkest distress and guilt, so that my natural eyes were not able to recognize or grasp anything more. Only the blind cry out to have their eyes opened.

Is, then, the one who prays this psalm, who prizes God's Word so highly, really a blind man? Certainly, whoever has glimpsed the wonderful word of God's law knows how blind he still is and how much he needs to have his eyes opened, lest he should sink again into deeper darkness.

It is our daily prayer each morning when our eyes open and the night is past that God should enlighten the eyes of our heart. We pray that they may stay open during the day when our natural eyes deceive us and the dreams of the night are replayed. Then may our enlightened eyes be always filled with the wonder of the law of God.

We must learn to do as the blind Bartimaeus did. When he heard that Jesus was on the street in Jericho and walking by him, he would allow no one to silence him but cried out for help until Jesus heard him. To the question, "What do you want me to do for you?" he answered at once, "Rabbi, I want to see." Thus he was healed (Mark 10:46–52). But with the blind man in Bethsaida (Mark 8:22–25) the healing was gradual and step-by-step, toward understanding and seeing. So are our eyes opened slowly and our understanding grows from a little knowledge to greater.

But whoever is confident that he can see, although he is blind, can no longer be helped but will perish in his blindness (John 9:40–41). It is a gift of grace for one to recognize his own blindness before the Word of God and to pray that his eyes be opened.

The one whose eyes God has opened to see the Word beholds a wonderland. What until then appeared to me as dead is now full of life, what was full of contradictions is resolved in a higher unity, the harsh demands become a gracious law. In the midst of human words, I hear God's eternal Word. In ancient stories I recognize the contemporary God and his work for my salvation.

God's comforting words become his new claim on me,
the unbearable burden becomes the easy yoke.

The great wonder in the law of God is the revelation
of the Lord Jesus Christ. Through him the Word receives
life: contradictions resolved, revelation of unimaginable
depths. Lord, open my eyes!

I am a stranger on earth;
do not hide your commands from me. (v. 19)

When I first encountered God's Word, it made me a
stranger upon the earth. It placed me among the long line
of our fathers in the faith, who dwelled as strangers in
the Promised Land (Hebrews 11:9). Abraham had faith
in the call that required him to leave his fatherland and
go to the Land of Promise; but in his old age, after the
death of Sarah, he had to bargain "as an alien and a
stranger" in this land, for a piece of land to "bury [his]
dead" (Genesis 23:4). Jacob confessed before Pharaoh
that his whole life had been a pilgrimage, shorter and
worse than that of his fathers, Abraham and Isaac (Genesis 47:9).

When the land of Canaan came into the possession of
the children of Israel, they were bidden never to forget
that they had been strangers and still were. They were
aliens in Egypt (Exodus 22:21) and to this day they are
"strangers and aliens" in the land, which belongs not to
them but to God (Leviticus 25:23). At the height of his

power, David included himself with these his forefathers when he said, "We are aliens and strangers in your sight, as were all our forefathers. Our days on earth are like a shadow, without hope" (1 Chronicles 29:15).

I am a stranger on earth. Thereby, I confess that I cannot remain here, that my time is short. Also that I have no freehold rights to land or house. All goods that come to me, I must receive thankfully. But I must suffer injustice and violence without retaliation. I must hold fast neither to man nor things.

As an alien, I am subject to the laws of my host country. The earth that nourishes me has a right to my labor and my strength. It is not for me to despise the earth on which I live. I owe it my trust and my thanks.

I may not put aside my lot as stranger and alien and thereby disregard the call of God to this alien status. I may not dream away my earthly life with thoughts of heaven. There is a very godless homesickness for the other world that prevents us from finding our home at all. I shall be a stranger with all that that involves. I shall not refuse to put my heart into the tasks, the pains, and the joys of earth. And I shall wait patiently for the redemption of the divine promise—really wait, and not rob my earthly life with wishes and dreams.

No word is said here about our true home. I know that this earth cannot be it and know that the earth is God's and that I am, even while on this earth, not only a stranger, but God's pilgrim and his alien (Psalm 39:12). But, because on earth I am nothing as a stranger, without rights, without support, without security, because God himself has made me weak and poor, therefore he has given me for my goal a pledge, unfailing: his Word. This one certainty he will not take away from me. This Word will hold me to him and will let me feel his power. When the Word is familiar and close to me, I can find my way in a strange land, my justice in injustice; my security in uncertainty; my strength in work; my patience in suffering. "Do not hide your commands from me." That is the prayer of the pilgrim in a strange land.

In truth, there is only one anxious thought that fills the stranger on earth, who has been called by the will of God and is an alien. It is that one day he will neither recognize or know the commands of God; what God requires him to do. And indeed in our personal lives or in his handling of historical events, God is often hidden. The worst fear is that the commands of God become so darkened that we discover nothing in the Word of God about what we should do. That is the temptation to doubt.

Even in the midst of our rejoicing in the law of the Lord, we are overwhelmed with fear: What if one day God should hide his commands from us? I would stumble into the abyss, with my first step I would fall, I would be destroyed in a strange land. Or—and this I really must ask myself—am I already living so much from my own standards that I would not even notice if God took his living law from me? Perhaps then I would continue to live by my own principles, but God's law would no longer be by me.

God's law is his personal word to me for the present day, for my daily life. It is not that God wants me to do this one day and something else the next. God's law is consistent within itself. But the decisive difference is whether I am obedient to my own principles or to God. If I am content with my own principles then I cannot understand the prayer of this psalmist. But if I know the way from God alone, then I live entirely by grace that he reveals or promises to me. Then I tremble at every word I receive from the mouth of God, waiting for the next word and proving the assurance of his grace. Thus, in all my ways and decisions, I remain utterly dependent upon grace and no false security can equal this living communion with God.

The cry that God may not hide his law from me comes from the heart that knows God's law. Without doubt, God has given us to know his law, and we have no excuse for not knowing his will. God does not allow us to live in unresolved conflict. He does not turn our life into an ethical tragedy, but he makes known to us his will. He supports us in fulfilling that law and punishes our disobedience.

In this matter, things are much simpler than we think. It is not that we do not know the law of God, but that we

do not do it—and then the inevitable consequences fol-
low such disobedience, that we no longer recognize his
law—that is our problem. Not that God hides his law
from us, but what is here meant is that God might call
down his grace upon us that his law would not be hidden from our eyes. It is within the freedom and wisdom
of God to withdraw the grace of his law from us. It is
then not for us to accept this with resignation, but rather
earnestly and ceaselessly pray: "Do not hide your commands from me."

My soul is consumed with longing
for your laws at all times. (v. 20)

The longing for God's commandments is greater than
our soul can bear. The soul is overwhelmed when from
God the great longing for his Word comes over us. This
longing to know God's commands, whatever it costs, is
not a strength to the soul but, on the contrary, its death.
It is not the soul with its manifold rules and desires, but
that which silences all other longings, the longing for
God's Word in me.

My soul cannot of itself fend off that thought which
comes again and again. To hear, to see, to recognize,
God's law rather than human rights, God's demands
rather than the claims of men, requires the total sacrifice
of the soul. When this longing for God comes over us,
the soul suffers torment, then it collapses. Then its lovely

systems melt away. He who goes on a pilgrimage does not ask about sweat and tears and the wounds he bears, he asks about the goal.

Because the longing for God's Word is not born in the soul, it is therefore not like a shaking or movement of the soul that is over in an hour or a day. It cannot be compared with the longing of the soul for a beloved person, because this is valid only for a period of time.

The longing for God that consumes the soul is true for all times. It cannot be otherwise when it comes over us from God himself. It must be forever. It has practically nothing to do with an emotional surge or single dedication of the heart to God's Word. It is a decision made for all time. Not the warmth of godliness but waiting upon the Word to the very end denotes a longing for the Word of God.

It is therefore wrong to confuse this longing with religious fervor. On the contrary, what we are talking about here is the experience of being consumed by the hunger of this longing. To see the just law of men triumph and, nonetheless, hope for the law of God. It is to allow oneself to live as an alien and yet not forget that we have a homeland. We cannot escape the knowledge that we live in sorrow, deprivation, and guilt before God. We seek him, where intellect and experience fail; when all powers are lost in death; then we experience God's Word as a powerful authority over our life, which will not let us go for an instant. This longing will last, unlike the exuberant joy of religious excitement. So, this "for all time" longing is not to be understood as a "mountaintop" experience, but as reality.

You rebuke the arrogant, who are cursed
and who stray from your commands. (v. 21)

God hates the proud, who are sufficient unto themselves and who pay no attention to divine or human laws. They give nothing for compassion and despise the words of God and his faithful. Pride before God is the root of all disobedience, all violence, all careless living. Pride is the source of all rebellion, all turmoil, all destruction. But after all, pride stands under a terrible threat of which the proud know nothing, but the faithful recognize "the gospel": "God opposes the proud but gives grace to the humble" (1 Peter 5:5).

God is with the weak and the humble—in a word, the cross of Jesus Christ is God's threat to the proud. They will be put to shame by God at the very moment when they think to have carried away the victory over all men.

Those who believe in the gospel see the sword of God over all the proud of the earth. The preaching of the Word of God is the only serious threat to a humanity that has become proud. God has also given the signs of his strength in his Word. In the course of history, here and there, God's threat comes to fruition, and the church sees with astonishment and awe, already in this time, the proud fallen and destroyed.

But let us beware of pharisaic security because we must recognize that the faithful may also be numbered with the proud and come under the certain judgment of God. All that may be hidden and dark, but the one thing that remains clear is that the Word declares a curse upon the ungodly: "Cursed are those who stray from thy commands." And in the Law it says, "Cursed is the man who does not uphold the words of this law by carrying them out" (Deuteronomy 27:26). Can we read these words without asking ourselves how it affects us? Should it not apply to us also, not only to others? The curse upon the breaking of God's commands is God's law and ... [here the manuscript breaks off][7]

Reasons for the Break

We cannot know why Bonhoeffer stopped in the middle of this sentence, at a point in his argument that was reaching a conclusion, albeit one that he himself had difficulty in reaching. The Psalms have always played a part in times of terror and persecution. The Covenanters in Scotland and the Dutch under the Spanish terror both found weapons in the Psalms. Bonhoeffer clearly refers to the German tyranny in his treatment of the proud, but he is conscious of his own situation at that moment and finds himself with a sense of guilt and dread that he too is about to break the commandments of God.

This part of his commentary was written in 1940, when he was aware of stepping into ethically uncertain grounds. On July 17, 1940, the news came of France's surrender, and there was rejoicing in Germany. Eberhard Bethge was with Bonhoeffer in Memel enjoying the sun when the news came over the loudspeaker that France had surrendered. The crowd stood up and cheered, singing the patriotic songs and raising their arms to Hitler. Bonhoeffer did the same and Bethge comments: "I stood there amazed. 'Raise your arm! Are you crazy!' he whispered to me, and later, 'We shall have to run risks for very different things now, but not for this salute!'"

"It was then that Bonhoeffer's double life began," writes Bethge.

Selections from *Ethics*

The Benedictine Monastery
at Ettal, Bavaria,
November 1940 –
February 1941

Psalms 9; 107; 148

BONHOEFFER, NOW IN THE EMPLOY OF THE ABWEHR, was part of the Conspiracy. He had been advised by the others that international pressure would topple the Nazi regime once the war started. But the victory of Germany's armies in France—brilliant and rapid, unlike the stalemate of 1914—left the conspirators and Bonhoeffer in confusion.

In the middle of July 1940, Bonhoeffer addressed a meeting of the Council of the Confessing Church about the situation and surprised them by what he said. He appeared, like everyone else in Germany, to have capitulated before Hitler's incredible success as before a divine judgment and recommended a new attitude towards the National Socialist State. This sounded as though he had changed sides and some present believed that. Wilhelm Rott, who was present, said, "It was clear to me that Bonhoeffer, who was always a good psychologist, described the situation so forcibly only so that we could deliver properly the old testimony that was required of us."

That summer and autumn Bonhoeffer had some new thinking to do. He was busy with his former students and much at home in Berlin, but in November 1940 he retired to the Benedictine Monastery in Ettal, Bavaria. He was on call from the Abwehr, which meant the Conspiracy, but until February 1941, he enjoyed a long period of rest and time for study. He also joined in the worship of the monastery, where his earlier writings were much respected and some read aloud at meals.

This new life as a political agent and a Lutheran pastor required very careful study and prayer. He expressed the opinion that what he was doing now might make it impossible for him to return to the ministry. At this time he worked steadily upon his book, later published in its unfinished form as *Ethics*.

Bethge tells us that the section Bonhoeffer worked on in these months was Luther's "Justification of the Sinner by Grace Alone." Although the justification is an act of God in Christ there is a preparation for this ultimate act, which he called the "penultimate." In his writing he depends much upon the Old Testament, particularly Isaiah, but also the Psalms. He writes:

> There is a depth of human bondage, of human poverty, of human ignorance, which impedes the merciful coming of Christ. If Christ is to come, then all that is proud and haughty must bow down. There is a measure of power, of wealth, of knowledge, which is an impediment to Christ. There is a measure of entanglement in the lie, in guilt, in one's own labor, in one's own work and in self love, which makes the coming of grace particularly difficult. That is why the way must be made straight by which Christ is to come to man.

Although the imagery of Isaiah 40 is there throughout, Bonhoeffer refers also to Psalm 9. Reading that section of the psalm, it is not difficult to see the relevance to what is happening in Hitler's victories and in Bonhoeffer's own hunger for righteousness. His acceptance of involvement in the political process made him unsure and searching for a new way: the sacrifice of his own righteousness. How far was this impeding the coming of Christ or preparing the way for grace.

PSALM 9:13–16

O LORD, *see how my enemies persecute me!*
  Have mercy and lift me up from the gates of death,
that I may declare your praises
    in the gates of the Daughter of Zion
    and there rejoice in your salvation.
The nations have fallen into the pit they have dug;
    their feet are caught in the net they have hidden.
The LORD is known by his justice;
    the wicked are ensnared by the work of their hands.

And as an answer to the unexpressed prayer that, if he is hindering the coming of grace by his involvement in sinful acts, the grace of God may break through, Bonhoeffer quotes, more than once, Psalm 107:15–16:

Let them give thanks to the LORD for his unfailing love
    and his wonderful deeds for men,
for he breaks down gates of bronze
    and cuts through bars of iron.

But on the positive side, Bonhoeffer was striving to fashion a Protestant ethic (in a Catholic monastery) which would match the situation of this monstrous tyranny. He rejected firmly the then prevalent view that "Protestant ethics is concerned with man's personality and with this personality alone. All the other things of this world remain untouched by this Protestant ethos." This is no obscure theological dispute. It raises the question, which for him now was personal:

> Is it the church's sole task to practice love and charity within the given worldly institutions, i.e., to inspire these institutions so far as possible with a new outlook, to mitigate hardship, to care for the victims of these institutions, and to establish a new order of her own within the congregation? Or, is the church charged with a mission towards the given worldly orders themselves, a mission of correction, improvement, etc., a mission to work towards a new worldly order? Has the church merely to gather up those whom the wheel has crushed or has she to prevent the wheel from crushing them? (*Ethics,* 287)

In this very important section, which he was working on in Ettal, he tackled the basic question of whether the commandments of God apply only to human beings and not to things: "Nature is subject to commandments which are revealed to us in the Word, the commandments of fruitfulness, of growth, etc."

His argument is clinched with Psalm 148. That glorious psalm of praise said it all. And he had in mind principally verses 3–6:

> *Praise him, sun and moon,*
> *praise him, all you shining stars.*
> *Praise him, you highest heavens*
> *and you waters above the skies.*
> *Let them praise the name of the* LORD,
> *for he commanded and they were created.*
> *He set them in place for ever and ever;*
> *he gave a decree that will never pass away.*

The singing of these psalms in the monastery deepened his love for them and later served him well in prison.

Letter to the Brethren at Finkenwalde

Advent Sunday 1942

Psalm 100

THE QUIETNESS OF THE BENEDICTINE MONASTERY came to an end in February 1941. Bonhoeffer was now fully working for the Abwehr. This gave him valid papers to visit neutral countries and those occupied and controlled by Germany. He made two visits to Switzerland and one to Scandinavia, where together with Helmuth von Moltke he stopped the planned execution of Eivind Berggrav, the bishop of Oslo. He conspired also to rescue several Jews and convey them to Switzerland, which followed directly after the first mass transportation of Jews from Berlin on October 16, 1941.

Events moved quickly in 1942. After the Japanese bombing of Pearl Harbor and the declaration of war by the U.S. at the end of 1941, the Conspiracy had new hope. At the end of May 1942, Bonhoeffer met Bishop Bell in Sweden and discussed the overthrow of the Nazi regime from within Germany. He asked Bell to convey to the British government the news that a powerful opposition was in place, able to accomplish this if Britain agreed to an honorable peace treaty. The efforts failed.

In September, "Operation 7," the transportation of the Jews to the safety of Switzerland, was successful; but Bonhoeffer's application for permits to visit the Balkans and Switzerland again was refused.

On November 24, he went to Pätzig to discuss his forthcoming engagement to Maria von Wedemeyer. A few days later he wrote a circular letter to his students, the "brethren" of the Finkenwalde community. It began with a recognition that many had died, mostly killed in action. Yet his theme was Psalm 100—not the most obvious psalm to use in a letter headed with a list of those killed in action.

PSALM 100

Shout for joy to the LORD, all the earth.
Worship the LORD with gladness;
come before him with joyful songs.
Know that the LORD is God.
It is he who made us, and we are his;
we are his people, the sheep of his pasture.

Enter his gates with thanksgiving
and his courts with praise;
give thanks to him and praise his name.
For the LORD is good and his love endures forever;
his faithfulness continues through all generations.

Advent Sunday 1942

Letter to the Brethren of Finkenwalde

Dear Brethren,

At the beginning of this letter which is to awaken you to the right kind of joy in serious times, we must list those who have been killed since last I wrote: P. Wilde, W. Brandenburg, Hermann Schroder, R. Lynker, Erwin Schutz, K. Rhode, Alfred Viol, Kurt Onnasch, to name the brethren. But also in addition—well known to many of you we must name Major von Wedemeyer and his oldest son, Max, whom I prepared some time ago for confirmation. "Everlasting joy will crown their heads." We shall not begrudge them that, indeed, sometimes in the stillness we shall envy them. From the earliest times in the Christian church, *acedia* [sorrow of the heart, resignation] has been one of the deadly sins. And so the psalmist bids us: "Serve the LORD with gladness."

Our life is given to us for this and for this reason we should hold to it still. The joy does not only belong to our call home at death but also to the life that we are living now, a joy that no one can take from us. In this joy, we are united with those who have been killed, not in sorrow. How can we help those who have become joyless and without courage if we are not ourselves bearers of courage and joy?

What is meant is not something artificially worked up or demanded of us but a gift freely given. Joy dwells in God and comes from him, possessing spirit, soul, and body. Once this joy has grasped a person, it grows, it carries him away, it throws open the closed doors. There is a joy that knows nothing of the heart's pain or need or anxiety; but it does not last, it can only drug one for a moment.

The joy of God has been through the poverty of the manger and the affliction of the cross; therefore, it is indestructible, irrefutable. It does not deny affliction when it is there, but it finds in the very midst of distress that God is there; it does not argue that sin is not griev-ous, but in that very place of sin is found forgiveness; it looks death in the face and it is just there that it finds life.

It is of this joy we speak, a joy which has overcome. It alone is credible, it alone helps and heals. The joy of those who have been called home is also the joy of over-coming—the Risen Lord bears the signs of the cross on his body. We stand in the midst of daily overcoming; they have for all time overcome. God alone knows how far or how near we stand to the final overcoming, in which by our own death we enter into joy:

> *Enter his gates with thanksgiving*
> *and his courts with praise.*

In the face of all the sorrows which these years have brought, many of us suffer a great deal from having our senses dulled. Recently, someone said to me, "I pray every day that I shall not become insensitive to what is going on." That is a good prayer. But we must be care-ful not to confuse our role with that of Christ. Christ endured suffering and all human guilt to the full; indeed he was Christ in that he suffered everything alone. Christ could suffer with people because he was able to redeem them from suffering. He has the power to suffer with people because of his love and his power to redeem them.

We are not called upon to burden ourselves with the sorrows of the whole world; we ourselves cannot suffer with others because we cannot redeem them. The desire to suffer with others in our own strength must be suppressed. We are only called to look with fullness of joy upon the one who really suffers with them and becomes their Redeemer. We may joyfully believe that there was, that there is, one to whom no human suffering and no human sin is strange, and who in the profoundest love has achieved our redemption. It is such joy in Christ, the Redeemer, that alone protects us from the dulling of our senses by the constant experience of human suffering and also from accepting as inevitable the suffering in the spirit of resignation.

For the LORD is good and his love endures forever;
his faithfulness continues through all generations.

The Prisoner

Tegel Prison, 1942

Psalm 47

1942–44

The First Years in Tegel Prison

The circular letter on joy in the midst of sorrow was a
fitting end to the year in which Bonhoeffer had played
his fullest role within the Conspiracy. He had hoped
against hope that there would be peace by negotiation
when the conspirators had overcome the deadly hold of
the Nazis on Germany. The year 1942 opened with the
ominous declaration by the Allies of "unconditional surrender"—the only possible peace terms (Casablanca,
January 14, 1942). That was the end of all peace-feelers.

A few days later, Bonhoeffer was engaged to be mar-
ried to Maria von Wedemeyer.

It was also a year of many abortive attempts to assassinate Hitler.

The last family celebration Bonhoeffer was able to
take part in was his father's seventy-fifth birthday on
March 31, 1942. The führer himself sent a greeting:

Hitler to Karl Bonhoeffer: In the name of the German
people I bestow on Professor Emeritus, Dr. Karl Bonhoeffer, the Goethe medal for Art and Science, insti-
tuted by the late Reich President Hindenberg.

A few days later, on April 5, Dietrich Bonhoeffer,
together with other members of his family, was arrested.
He was taken to Tegel Prison in Berlin, where after some

initial unpleasantness, he managed to adapt to prison life; he was to spend the rest of his life in prison.

He wrote letters to his fiancée, his parents, but most of all to his friend and colleague, Eberhard Bethge.

The Prisoner

At first, Bonhoeffer found the prison cell revolting and dirty. The shock and the uncertainty as to why he was there left him bewildered. He gradually worked out a pattern of life but stressed that it was not a good thing to accept prison life as normal. A former prisoner had scribbled on the wall, "In a hundred years it will all be over." That was a way of dealing with time that Bonhoeffer rejected.

He turned to the Psalms in his attempt to come to terms with time. Writing to his parents in the middle of May—almost six weeks after his arrest—he expressed the wish to talk over his reactions with his father, a distinguished psychologist; adding that from Psalm 31, "My times are in your hands" is the Bible answer, but from Psalm 13 he quoted a question that dominates everything: "How long, O LORD?"

In that same letter, he writes:

> I am reading the Bible straight through from cover to cover, and have just got as far as Job, which I am particularly fond of. I read the Psalms every day, as I

have done for years; I know them and love them more
than any other book.

He makes mention then of three Psalms—3, 47,
and 70.

PSALM 47

Clap your hands, all you nations;
    shout to God with cries of joy.
How awesome is the LORD Most High,
    the great King over all the earth!
He subdued nations under us,
    peoples under our feet.
He chose our inheritance for us,
    the pride of Jacob, whom he loved.   *Selah*

God has ascended amid shouts of joy,
    the LORD amid the sounding of trumpets.
Sing praises to God, sing praises;
    sing praises to our King, sing praises.

For God is the King of all the earth;
    sing to him a psalm of praise.
God reigns over the nations;
    God is seated on his holy throne.
The nobles of the nations assemble
    as the people of the God of Abraham,
for the kings of the earth belong to God;
    he is greatly exalted.

Particularly of this psalm, but also Psalms 3 and 70, he says:

> I cannot now read Psalms 3, 47, and 70, and others without hearing them in the settings by Heinrich Schutz. It was Renate [his niece and about to be married to his closest friend, Eberhard Bethge] who introduced me to his music, and I count it one of the greatest enrichments of my life.

Like so many others, Bonhoeffer felt that the Psalms were inextricably bound up with music. Months later, Psalm 47 and the music of Schutz were still enriching his life. He wrote to Eberhard Bethge on November 20,

> There is nothing I miss here—except all of you. I wish I could play the G Minor sonata with you and sing some Schutz, and hear you sing Psalms 70 and 47; that was what you did best.

Eberhard Bethge, while he lived, was our primary source of Bonhoeffer's inner feelings. Commenting upon a new issue of the book that was the last to be published in Bonhoeffer's lifetime, *Das Gebetbuch der Bibel,* Bethge writes:

> It is good that this new edition publishes once again the David picture. Not only because this much loved sculpture from Worms shows David playing the harp to his psalms, but also because it pushes to the background all the historical and critical doubts about

David the psalmist and brings forward the role of these prayers for the Christian. For him, it was not the historical background of these old poems that was important but the continuity of the experience of salvation which the children of God find in praying of the psalms and their connection with the lineage of Christ and his promise.

Meditation from the *Losungen* for May 29, 1944

Tegel Prison, Whitsun 1944

Psalm 94

THE FESTIVAL OF WHITSUN had always meant a great deal to Bonhoeffer—especially in the seminary at Finkenwalde. "Eberhard," he writes, "is the recollection of Whit Sunday morning at Finkenwalde as splendid and as important for you as it is for me?" It was at Whitsuntide two years earlier that he had met with the bishop of Chichester in Sweden and laid before him plans for the overthrow of the Nazi regime, asking for a word of encouragement from Britain. Shortly before Whitsun 1944, Eberhard and Renate had their first child and Bonhoeffer, who could not attend the baptism of the baby—called Dietrich—sent a baptismal sermon, which is one of his most important statements about the future of the church.

Shortly after that he had tried to help Bethge in personal problems, but eventually sent to him comments upon the *Losungen* passages for the days of Whitsun: May 28–30, 1944. Not all the passages are from the Psalms. They are:

May 28—Isaiah 57:18 and Galatians 4:6
May 29—Psalm 94:12–13 and Galatians 5:22
May 30—Genesis 39:23 and 1 John 3:24

It is the middle one that is important for our purposes.

PSALM 94:12–13

Blessed is the man you discipline, O LORD,
*   the man you teach from your law;*
you grant him relief from days of trouble,
*   till a pit is dug for the wicked.*

Luther's translation is:

Blessed is the man you discipline, O LORD,
*   the man you teach from your law;*
that he might have patience when evil triumphs.

Meditation from the *Losungen*
for May 29, 1944

Blessed is the man you discipline . . . that he might have
patience when evil triumphs.

Almost the whole of our innermost worries in recent
times seems to be summed up there. How can we reach
that state of mind? When God's blows fall upon us and
his law is heavy, can we learn to say, "Blessed is the man
to whom this befalls"? Yes, we who call God "loving
Father" must say this.

Whom God disciplines through hard experiences of
life, through war and deprivation, learns that he has no

right to expect anything from God and simply waits humbly and patiently until God smiles upon him again as he turns to him; he knows that the hour will come. When God lays the full weight of his law upon a man, he knows that he is guilty, sharing the guilt of all men, and he prepares himself in patience and obedience, doing nothing but waiting and praying. In bearing the punishment and obediently accepting God's will we know that we are being disciplined by the hand of the loving Father and say, "Blessed is the man you discipline."

But for us there is always the danger that patience is looked upon as the only and most important Christian attitude, and thereby we limit the rule of God. It is in the times of persecution that the fullness of the Holy Spirit unfolds and matures, and we should make room in ourselves for what God wants, what men want, and what we ourselves want. That the whole world of God, the loving Father, would be born, grow, and mature in us.

These are the fruits of the Spirit: love—where only mistrust and hatred rule; joy—in place of bitterness and pain; peace—where there is inner and public strife; patience—where impatience threatens to overwhelm us; kindness—where only rough and harsh words are apparently given weight; goodness—where understanding and sympathy are reckoned as weaknesses; faithfulness (which means loyalty) where divisions and great changes have shattered the most long-standing relationships;

gentleness—where thoughtlessness and selfishness appear to be the way to get on; self-control—where brief pleasures appear to be all that matter and all moral restraint is lost (Galatians 5:22–23).

Is this all fantastic illusion? Is it impossible? It would be if it were not growing entirely as fruit from the Spirit himself, whom we have entreated and who will bring all this to fruition in us, while we, astounded and humble, let the Spirit work in us.[8]

Meditations
from the *Losungen*
for June 7 and 8, 1944

Tegel Prison
After Whitsun 1944

Psalms 54; 34

THE DAYS FOLLOWING WHITSUN 1944 mark a change or development in Bonhoeffer's attitude. Before Whitsun, he had written the baptismal sermon for the young Dietrich Bethge and encouraged Eberhard to enjoy his leave with Renate. He now began to feel the separation from family and friends more intensely. What he had written for Bethge on the *Losungen* for Whitsun became very much his own support.

He had news of attempts to be made on the life of Adolf Hitler. After the failure of the British to respond to the offer that Bonhoeffer had brought to the bishop of Chichester in Sweden, the military had formed their own resistance, and failed attempts were made to assassinate Hitler. Great store was set by an attempt to be made on July 20, 1944.

In this period, Bonhoeffer depended much upon his inner resources and did not find it easy. He began to write poetry, describing his struggles with himself and with his God (that poetry is collected in the volume *Dietrich Bonhoeffer's Prison Poems,* Zondervan, 2005). He analyzed himself, and as one poem shows, he recognized a distinct difference between what people thought of him and what he knew himself to be ("Who Am I?").

The fortunes of war were turning against Germany and the bombing of Berlin became more intense. Somewhat dryly he writes, "We're getting up at 1:30 A.M. almost every night here; it's a bad time, and it handicaps work rather." Earlier, he tried to assess his attitude during a bombing raid: "One gradually learns to acquire an inner detachment from life's menaces—although 'acquire detachment' seems too negative, formal, artificial, and stoical; and it's perhaps more accurate to say that we assimilate these menaces into our life as a whole. I notice repeatedly how few people there are who can harbor conflicting emotions at the same time." What follows is an unsympathetic comment upon the behavior of his fellow prisoners in an air raid! Then, "They miss the fullness of life and the wholeness of an independent existence; everything objective and subjective is dissolved for them into fragments." He contrasts this with Christianity "which puts us into many different dimensions of life at the same time; we make room for ourselves, to some extent, for God and the whole world."

A week later Bonhoeffer confessed to Bethge that he was writing poetry and sent him a copy of *"Vergangenheit"* ("Past"). Other poems followed. About the same time he sent Bethge a further meditation upon the *Losungen* for June 7 and 8, 1944. The Bible readings are:

Psalm 54:4; 1 Thessalonians 5:23
Psalm 34:19; 1 Peter 3:9

Meditations from the *Losungen*
for June 7 and 8, 1944

Surely God is my help;
  the Lord is the one who sustains me.

Psalm 54:4

The first time that the Bible speaks of a "helper" is the creation of Eve: "I will make a helper suitable for him," God says to Adam. Perhaps this word has appeared to us in happier times too narrowly as describing what marriage is.

If we look much later in the Bible, namely at the farewell discourses of Jesus in John's gospel, the word *helper* is the one whom Jesus will send to those he is leaving behind in the world, from his heavenly state. We read, "I will ask the Father, and he will give you another Counselor [which is really our word *helper*] to be with you forever" (John 14:16). In this that first word from the creation story is fulfilled in an immeasurably higher sense.

You are my helper for body, soul, and spirit; I trust you with my body, soul, and spirit—that is what we say in the marriage ceremony when God has joined man and wife for one another. Together they do a divine work, although they are only earthly creatures. It is God himself who takes this work into his hands and completes it through the Holy Spirit.

We understand that this helper is the essence of marriage most clearly when it appears that we must make sacrifices. We will sacrifice everything else—joy, pleasure, success—gladly if we can but help one another. Nothing is harder for us than when the other is in danger, has hard work, difficult decisions, painful circumstances, and must face all this alone, while we cannot help him; that is what makes separation in marriage so hard. In such a situation, the word of the psalmist comes to us: "Surely God is my help."

This is what one says to the other, as he trusts the other and himself to God. He knows all that God has done for him in the past, he knows that God was true and remained true, that he had never and that he never would leave him without a helper in dangers and difficulties.

Can we support one another better, can we help one another more, than when with confidence and certainty we say to one another: "Don't worry about me, I am cared for! Have no fear, I am not left alone! 'Surely God is my help!' Be comforted and I will be comforted! Wherever I am, the Lord stands by me and helps me. And he is the one who sustains me. 'Surely the Lord is my help.' With all our efforts, ideas, and concerns we could not sustain our life for a single day, but the Lord who commands all the world and sets all things in motion, can turn around every danger. He 'has many thousand ways

to rescue us from death' [a line from a hymn by Paul Ger-
hardt]. He alone sustains my life. 'For he will command
his angels concerning you to guard you in all your ways'
(Psalm 91:11)." Thus should we speak to one another
and not of all the other things that disturb and threaten
us. "Surely God is my help."

Does this mean that we have to stop caring for one
another? Certainly not. But it is true that we cannot help
the other if God does not help us. Insofar as we continue
to remember that, we help ourselves.

Is that unreal? No, when with full trust and certainty
of faith, we commit one another to God, who helps us,
and thereby comfort one another, then even the time of
separation is a help, a comfort for the body, for the soul,
and for the spirit. We remain fast bound to each other
with body, soul, and spirit, and thus fulfil the Word of
Creation: "I will make a helper for you."

What is the purpose of all this? It is to prepare for the
Day of Jesus Christ, the Day of his future. By his will,
God has given us our marriage; by his will, we stand by
each other; by his will, God stands by us and preserves
us. By his will, he presents our body, our soul, our spirit
"faultless," so that we with body, soul, and spirit can
stand before God through all eternity.

As one, whether we are together or separated, we
move towards this goal. On the way there, we help each
other and commit one another to him who alone can pre-

serve us, and who throughout eternity will transfigure our body, our soul, and our spirit into a new eternal life. Then, though ashamed but thankful, we shall say, "God stands by me." Amen.

A righteous man may have many troubles,
    but the LORD delivers him from them all.

                                                        Psalm 34:19

The righteous man suffers within the world, the unrighteous man does not. The righteous man suffers from things that for others are taken for granted and necessary. The righteous man suffers in the face of unrighteousness, of meaninglessness, and of wrong; he suffers when the divine orders of marriage and the family are destroyed. He suffers in this way not only because he sees in all this a great loss but also because he recognizes something ungodly.

The world says, "It has always been like this and must be so." The righteous man says, "It should not be so, it is against God." That is how you recognize a righteous man, that he suffers in this world. One may say that in a way he brings the perception of God into the world; therefore like God, he suffers in the world— "But the LORD delivers him."

Not all human suffering is helped by God. But in the suffering of the righteous there is always God's help, because he suffers with God. God is always by him. The righteous man knows that God lets him suffer in this way in order that he may learn to love God of his own will. The righteous man finds God in his suffering. That is his help. Find God in your separation and you find your help.

The answer of the righteous man to the suffering that the world inflicts upon him is called blessing. That was the answer of God to the world that slew Christ on the cross—blessing. God does not repay like with like, and neither should the righteous man do so. Not to condemn, not to curse, but to bless. There would be no hope for the world if this were not so. The world lives from the blessing of God and of the righteous and by this blessing it has a future.

Blessing means to lay the hand upon the shoulder and say, "Despite everything you belong to God." That is how we deal with the world that inflicts so much suffering upon us. We don't give it up, reject it, or despise it; we do not damn it; we call it to God; we give it hope; we lay our hand upon it and say, "May God's blessings come upon you, he will renew you, blessings on you, you were created by God, to whom you belong, for he is your Creator and your Redeemer."

We have received God's blessing in joy and in sorrow. But we who have been ourselves blessed can do no other than pass on this blessing. Yes, the righteous man must be a blessing, there where he is. Only by the impossible can the world be renewed and God's blessing is the impossible.

When Jesus ascended into heaven, "he lifted up his hands and blessed them [the disciples]" (Luke 24:50). We hear him in this hour speaking to us and saying:

> *The LORD bless you and keep you;*
>   *the LORD make his face shine upon you and be*
>   *gracious to you;*
> *the LORD turn his face toward you and give you peace.*
>   Numbers 6:24–26

Amen.[9]

The Plot That Failed: Letters to Eberhard and Renate Bethge

Tegel Prison,
July 20 and 21, 1944

Various Psalms

THIS MEDITATION WAS INTENDED SPECIFICALLY FOR EBERHARD and Renate Bethge. Bonhoeffer had heard of the difficulties Eberhard had in coming to terms with separation from Renate and their newly born son: Bethge was on the Italian front and had been anxious about leave to attend the baptism of his child.

Bonhoeffer wrote:

Dear Eberhard, dear Renate!

These words flow from my pen as I meditate upon the *Losungen* for the following days with you. They have been thrown together in a hurry and not carefully formulated and will only have value with your own reading of the text. They may possibly be helpful. I had the courage to send them to you only because you said that the meditations I sent at Whitsun had pleased you. Now, keep well, be of good faith and hope with me for another happy meeting very soon.

The Plot That Failed

However reluctantly, Bonhoeffer was involved in the plots to assassinate Hitler. There were several attempts, even before Bonhoeffer was arrested, and he watched their repeated failures with disappointment. In prison, he was kept informed by coded messages. He was anxiously awaiting the news of a plot that looked to have every prospect of success. It failed, but we do not know how soon Bonhoeffer knew of the failure.

On July 21, he wrote to Bethge, saying that the long theological discussions they had been having by letter would pause for a while. He writes,

> These theological thoughts are, in fact, always occupying my mind; but there are times when I am just content to live the life of faith without worrying about its problems. At those times, I simply take pleasure in the day's readings—in particular those of yesterday and today [i.e. July 20 and 21].

On each of those days, there is a verse from the Psalms.

(July 20)
Some trust in chariots and some in horses,
 but we trust in the name of the LORD our God.

Psalm 20:7

(July 21)
The Lord is my shepherd,
 I shall not be in want.

Psalm 23:1

Bonhoeffer's constant reading of the Psalms meant that very often they needed no commentary—they spoke directly to the situation.

In this letter of July 21 he recalls an incident in New York thirteen years earlier—a conversation with Jean Lasserre, a French fellow student in Union Theological

Seminary. Lasserre had said that he would like to become a saint. Bonhoeffer had said that he "should like to learn to have faith." Thirteen years had passed and Bonhoeffer stood by that statement, adding that he now knew that "it is only by living completely in this world that one learns to have faith." He expands this with,

> By this worldliness I mean living unreservedly in life's duties, problems, successes and failures, experiences and perplexities. In so doing we throw ourselves completely into the arms of God, taking seriously, not our own sufferings, but those of God in the world—watching with Christ in Gethsemane. That, I think, is faith, that is how one becomes a man and a Christian. How can success make us arrogant or failure lead us astray, when we share in God's suffering through a life of this kind?

A few days earlier, he had suggested to Bethge some texts he might use if he had to preach in the difficult conditions of the Italian front. Three of them are from the Psalms:

My soul finds rest in God alone; my salvation comes from him. (62:1)
Save me, for I am yours. (119:94)
Why are you downcast, O my soul? Why so disturbed within me? (42:5)

These texts are so obviously relevant to the waiting situation; it cannot have been very long before Bonhoeffer heard of the failure of the plot.

His attention seems now to turn to the poetry he is writing, in particular the poem "Voices in the Night." He repeatedly asks Bethge if he has read the poem. In fact, he seems anxious about all the poems. "Success and Failure" is his meditation upon the difference either would make in the outcome. He seems almost to feel that failure could be less harmful than success. But this is before he has heard of the failure and the subsequent hunt for the conspirators involved, which led to a massive and cruel purge of all who were opposed to the Nazi regime.

In this period before and after July 20, Bonhoeffer sought to express himself in prose (two fragments of a novel survive) and in drama (a fragment of a play survives), but it is in poetry where he found release. Only two of the poems are biblical—both Old Testament: "The Death of Moses" and "Jonah."

All ten poems are much concerned with his own state of mind. In "Moses" he sees his life work incomplete. He had returned to Germany that he might participate in the reconstruction of church and state after the war. It now looked as though he would not survive. Like Moses, he did not enter the Promised Land but died in sight of it.

His anxieties had been expressed many times in his letters, but now he found poetry the medium for so explosive a theme.

The Psalms Echoed in Bonhoeffer's Poetry

Tegel Prison, 1944

Psalms 3; 47; 70

THE PSALMS SEEMED TO SPEAK FOR BONHOEFFER—his longing for deliverance, his sense of guilt, his confidence in God. While he was fond of Job, and surely there were times when he uttered the cry, "Though he slay me, yet will I trust in him" (13:15 KJV), it is, however, the Psalms that echo in his poetry. Earlier he had said that he could not read Psalms 3, 47, and 70 without hearing the music of Heinrich Schutz. These three psalms illustrate this connection with his poems.

PSALM 3

O LORD, *how many are my foes!*
  How many rise up against me!
Many are saying of me,
  "God will not deliver him."   Selah

But you are a shield around me, O LORD;
  you bestow glory on me and lift up my head.
To the LORD I cry aloud,
  and he answers me from his holy hill.   Selah

I lie down and sleep;
  I wake again, because the LORD sustains me.
I will not fear the tens of thousands
  drawn up against me on every side.

Arise, O LORD!
  Deliver me, O my God!

Strike all my enemies on the jaw;
  break the teeth of the wicked.

From the LORD comes deliverance.
  May your blessing be on your people.   *Selah*

Bonhoeffer's Poetry

Bonhoeffer's poem "Voices in the Night" is one of terrible introspection during the cold hours of darkness. It sets the scene of hopelessness and guilt, but like the psalmist cries out for God's deliverance:

Lord, after the ferment of these days,
send us times to prove us.
After so much wrong,
let us see the day dawn! . . .

We will prepare ourselves in quietness
until you call us to new times.
Until you still the storm and abate the flood,
and your will works wonders.

The tone is different, but the cry is the same. It comes again in his last poem, "By Kindly Powers Surrounded":

Though from the old our hearts are still in pain,
while evil days oppress with burdens still,
Lord, give to our frightened souls again,
salvation and thy promises fulfill.

Search these poems and you will hear that psalmist's cry that Bonhoeffer could not erase from his memory.

PSALM 47

Clap your hands, all you nations;
shout to God with cries of joy.
How awesome is the LORD Most High,
the great King over all the earth!
He subdued nations under us,
peoples under our feet.
He chose our inheritance for us,
the pride of Jacob, whom he loved.   *Selah*

God has ascended amid shouts of joy,
the LORD amid the sounding of trumpets.
Sing praises to God, sing praises;
sing praises to our King, sing praises.

For God is the King of all the earth;
sing to him a psalm of praise.
God reigns over the nations;
God is seated on his holy throne.
The nobles of the nations assemble
as the people of the God of Abraham,
for the kings of the earth belong to God;
he is greatly exalted.

Inevitably this psalm surfaces in the long poem "The Death of Moses." Moses accepts God's judgment that he should see the Promised Land but not enter it. An acceptance that Bonhoeffer strove to understand. But in the course of following Moses' vision of the future, Bonhoeffer writes:

To you, Lord, we will the offering bring,
and to you the songs of salvation sing.

In thanks and rejoicing with one voice,
may your people proclaim they are your choice.

The world is great; it stretches to the sky,
people behold, as they in deep confusion lie.

In your Word, which you to us make known,
to all peoples you have the way to life now shown.

Always, the world will in days of heavy task,
of your holy ten commandments ask.

Always, a people, however guilty they be,
alone in your holiness will healing see.

And thus my people are called with attractions fair,
to the free land and the free air.

Possess the mountains and the fertile lands,
blest by your fathers' godly hands,

Wipe from their brow the hot desert sand
and breathe freedom in the promised land.

In this poem, Bonhoeffer has identified his vision of the world assembled as the people of the God of Abraham. It is extraordinary that a man so near to a death that would rob him of all his longing for the future in a restored Germany can sing the praises of Psalm 47 and like Moses rejoice.

And it comes again in his last poem—a Gethsemane poem, in which, like Moses, he accepts the "bitter cup" but prays that it might pass from him. After accepting God's will, he praises with a vision from Psalm 47:

Let candles burn, both warm and bright,
Which to our darkness thou has brought, . . .
When we are wrapped in silence most profound,
May we hear that song most fully raised
From all the unseen world that lies around
And thou art by all thy children praised. . . .
Night and morning, God is by us faithfully
And surely at each newborn day.

PSALM 70

Hasten, O God, to save me;
*   O LORD, come quickly to help me.*
May those who seek my life
*   be put to shame and confusion;*
may all who desire my ruin
*   be turned back in disgrace.*

> *May those who say to me, "Aha! Aha!"*
> *turn back because of their shame.*
> *But may all who seek you*
>   *rejoice and be glad in you;*
> *may those who love your salvation always say,*
>   *"Let God be exalted!"*
>
> *Yet I am poor and needy;*
>   *come quickly to me, O God.*
> *You are my help and my deliverer;*
>   *O LORD, do not delay.*

If our image of Bonhoeffer does not fit an anxious prayer like that, it is because we are among those who observe him from the outside. In his poem "Who Am I?" he shows that contrast:

> *Who am I? They often tell me,*
> *I step out from my cell,*
> *composed, contented and sure,*
> *like a lord from his manor. . . .*
>
> *Am I really what others tell me?*
> *Or am I only what I myself know of me?*
> *Troubled, homesick, ill like a bird in a cage,*
> *gasping for breath, as though one strangled me,*
> *hungering for colors, for flowers, for songs of birds,*
> *thirsting for kind words, for human company . . .*
> *empty and tired of praying, of thinking, or working,*
> *exhausted and ready to bid farewell to it all.*

That poet could pray like the psalmist.

The psalm looks in two directions—toward God who can deliver and toward the enemy who must be defied. This is matched by a section in "Voices in the Night":

I will see the times change,
when signs light up the heavens,
new bells ring over the people,
growing louder and louder.

I wait for that midnight,
in which the shining splendor
dazzles and destroys the evil in our fear,
to establish with joy that which is right . . .

Suddenly, I wake up,
as though, from a sinking ship, I sighted land,
as though there was something firm to grasp,
as though fruit was ripening to gold.
But when I look, grasp or hold,
there is only an impenetrable mass of darkness.

I sink into brooding,
I lower myself into the heart of darkness.
You, night, full of horror and evil,
make yourself known to me!
Why and how long will you gnaw at our patience? . . .

Though robbed of freedom and honor,
we stand tall before men with pride.
And when we are wrongly decried,
before men we declare our innocence freely ...

Only before Thee, maker of all,
before Thee alone are we sinners.

These late poems bring Bonhoeffer closer than ever to
the songs and prayers, the protests and the longings of
the book of Psalms. Here he proved the truth of his own
words long before:

> There is not a single detail of the piety and impiety of
> the Christian church that is not found in the Psalms
> and to study them is to make a strange journey of ups
> and downs, falling and rising, despair and exaltation,
> the experience of those who pray their way through
> the Psalms, one after the other.

And this he did until the Psalms interpreted his prayers
and, like Luther, he became aware that in them he could
hear the voice of Christ praying with him and for him.

The End— and a Beginning: More Poetry

Prinz Albrecht Strasse, Buchenwald, and Flossenburg Prisons, 1944

Psalm 22

ON SEPTEMBER 22, 1944, DOCUMENTS were discovered at the emergency headquarters of the Abwehr in Zossen that incriminated many of Bonhoeffer's family as well as himself. It put an end to his comparatively free life in the Tegel prison, where he could receive books and paper and even visitors. There he had been able to prepare a plan of escape, which was ready and would have been successful on October 5. But the Zossen papers made it fairly certain that had he tried to escape, his family would have suffered, so he abandoned the plan and his transfer to the Gestapo bunker in Prinz Albrecht Strasse made any future plans impossible.

Until he left the prison in Tegel, he could still contemplate survival. Now he faced the near certainty of death as well as a sense of guilt. This comes out most clearly in two poems, "The Sacrifice of Jonah" and "The Death of Moses." They both echo the same sense of guilt expressed in so many of the Psalms.

> *Thus they prayed and Jonah spoke, "I am the man!*
> *My life is forfeit. I opposed God's will."*

> *"Cast me out, my guilt incurs God's anger still.*
> *The righteous should not perish with wrong!"*
> (from "Jonah," written just before he left Tegel)

> *Doubting and impatient thought*
> *almost brought my faith to nought.*

> *You forgive, but 'tis a blazing fire*
> *to stand before the Truth, a liar.*

Your nearness and of your face the sight
are to the penitent, a wounding light.

Your sadness and your great scorn
bury into my flesh, a deadly thorn.

Before your holy word, which you inflamed,
that which I preached, I am ashamed.

(from "The Death of Moses")

There are many other places in the poems where guilt
is recognized before God. In the Psalms, the cry for God's
deliverance is often followed by a recognition of guilt and
fear that God has forgotten the psalmist. The most obvious is Psalm 22, which must often have been recalled by
Bonhoeffer:

PSALM 22

My God, my God, why have you forsaken me?
  Why are you so far from saving me,
  so far from the words of my groaning?
O my God, I cry out by day, but you do not answer.

vv. 1–2

Followed by the memory that:

In you our fathers put their trust;
  they trusted and you delivered them.
They cried to you and were saved;
  in you they trusted and were not disappointed.

vv. 4–5

There follows a section that is echoed in the poem "Voices in the Night" during the cold hours of the night:

All who see me mock me;
   they hurl insults, shaking their heads:
He trusts in the LORD;
   let the LORD rescue him.
Let him deliver him,
   since he delights in him.

vv. 7–8

The whole psalm, no doubt remembered by heart, must have forced him to the dilemma: why? But the psalm does not end in despair. The future belongs to God:

Posterity will serve him;
   future generations will be told about the Lord.
They will proclaim his righteousness
   to a people yet unborn—
   for he has done it.

vv. 30–31

PRINZ ALBRECHT STRASSE

That triumph comes in his last poem, written in Prinz Albrecht Strasse:

And shouldst thou offer us the bitter cup, resembling
sorrow, filled to the brim and overflowing,

we will receive it thankfully, without trembling,
from thy hand so good and ever-loving.

And in a later stanza,

When we are wrapped in silence most profound,
may we hear that song most fully raised
from all the unseen world that lies around
and thou art by all thy children praised.

He did not remain in the Gestapo bunker in Prinz Albrecht Strasse. The Russians were advancing towards Berlin, and together with other important prisoners, he was moved from place to place. After a very heavy bombing raid on Berlin, February 3, 1945, twenty of these prisoners, including Bonhoeffer, were sent away from Berlin. Bonhoeffer with several of the conspirators went to Thüringia and the concentration camp at Buchenwald. It was there that the first martyr of the Confessing Church was executed. Bonhoeffer and the others were "housed" in the damp air-raid shelter cells. They stayed there five weeks and then were on the move again. Bonhoeffer's fiancée, Maria von Wedemeyer, traveled from camp to camp, searching in vain for her Dietrich.

On Easter Day, April 1, the prisoners could hear the American guns and knew that the war was virtually over. Germany would have to admit defeat. Surely all the trials would be abandoned under such circumstances. But they were not. On the way to Flossenburg, they stopped at a school where the special prisoners were placed in a schoolroom. The easy atmosphere there enabled Bonhoeffer to conduct a church service on Sunday, April 8, Low Sunday. Catholics and one atheist (Wasily Wasiliev Kokorin, Molotov's nephew) joined in. The text was given and Bonhoeffer preached from it:

> *Praise be to the God and Father of our Lord Jesus Christ! In his great mercy he has given us new birth into a living hope through the resurrection of Jesus Christ from the dead ...*
>
> 1 Peter 1:3

> *... and by his wounds we are healed.*
>
> Isaiah 53:5

That evening they arrived in Flossenburg for the trials that would condemn some to death by hanging—painfully.

Bonhoeffer's own poem "Stages on the Way to Freedom" ends with death as the last stage:

> *Come now, highest feast on the way to everlasting freedom,*
> *death. Lay waste the burdens of chains and walls*
> *which confine our earthly bodies and blinded souls,*
> *that we see at last what here we could not see.*
> *Freedom, we sought you long in discipline, action, and suffering.*
> *Dying, we recognize you now in the face of God.*

In the gray dawn of Monday, April 9, Bonhoeffer was called to his execution. Before he went, he asked Captain Payne Best, a fellow prisoner more likely to survive, to remember him to the bishop of Chichester. His last words were, "This is the end—for me the beginning of life."

Sources

1. Bonhoeffer, *Werke Vol. 9*, abbreviated, 510–16.
2. Bonhoeffer, *Werke Vol. 10*, abbreviated, 479–85.
3. Bonhoeffer, *Werke Vol. 11*, 377–85.
4. Bonhoeffer, *Werke Vol. 13*, 298–301—
   original in English.
5. Bonhoeffer, *Werke Vol. 14*, 980–88.
6. Bonhoeffer, *Werke Vol. 15*, 15–19.
7. Bonhoeffer, *Werke Vol. 15*, 499–535.
   His commentary on all three sections.
8. Bonhoeffer, *Werke Vol. 16*, 652–53.
9. Bonhoeffer, *Werke Vol. 16*, 654–58.

Dietrich Bonhoeffer's Prison Poems

Editor and Translator
Edwin Robertson

This book contains the powerful, personal, and deeply moving poetry written by Dietrich Bonhoeffer, one of the most important Christian writers and martyrs of the century. From his prison cell, where he awaited execution for conspiring to assassinate Adolf Hitler, Bonhoeffer wrote ten powerful poems, charged with the white-hot emotions and disarming candor of a man who lived and ultimately died by the truth.

Hardcover: 0-310-26704-8

Pick up a copy today at your favorite bookstore!

ZONDERVAN™

GRAND RAPIDS, MICHIGAN 49530 USA

WWW.ZONDERVAN.COM

We want to hear from you. Please send your comments about this book to us in care of zreview@zondervan.com. Thank you.

ZONDERVAN™

GRAND RAPIDS, MICHIGAN 49530 USA

WWW.ZONDERVAN.COM